Joseph Hamilton Fesperman, F. W. E. Peschau

The Life of a Sufferer

An Autobiography

Joseph Hamilton Fesperman, F. W. E. Peschau

The Life of a Sufferer
An Autobiography

ISBN/EAN: 9783337117719

Printed in Europe, USA, Canada, Australia, Japan

Cover: Foto ©ninafisch / pixelio.de

More available books at **www.hansebooks.com**

THE LIFE OF A SUFFERER:

An Autobiography

BY

Rev. JOSEPH HAMILTON FESPERMAN.

"What I do thou knowest not now;
but thou shalt know hereafter."
—*St. John 13: 7.*

"Even so, Father, for so it
seemed good in Thy sight."
—*St. Luke 10: 21.*

With an Introduction by

REV. F. W. E. PESCHAU, D. D.,

Pastor St. Paul's Evangelical Lutheran Church, Wilmington, N. C., and Associate Editor of The Lutheran Visitor.

Published for the Author by
THE YOUNG LUTHERAN COMPANY,
UTICA, N. Y.

L. C. CHILDS & SON,
PRINTERS AND BINDERS,
UTICA, N. Y.

TO
MY DEVOTED WIFE
WHOSE TRUE HEART HAS NEVER FALTERED
AND WHOSE GENTLE FOOTSTEPS
HAVE NEVER WEARIED
IN THE PATHWAY OF LOVE
FOR TWENTY AND SIX YEARS,
IS THIS VOLUME LOVINGLY DEDICATED
BY AN
AFFECTIONATE HUSBAND.

PREFACE.

In venturing to give this work to the public, the author complies with repeated and earnest solicitations, and he owes it to those who may become his readers, not less than to himself, to explain the circumstances under which the book was prepared.

In September, 1891, when he was making arrangements to visit Baltimore, Md., to undergo a critical surgical operation, he was advised by physicians, ministers, and laymen to defer the operation, and was requested to write an account of his birth, education, ministry, misfortunes and varied afflictions. Believing the desire of his friends to be an indication of the will of God, he commenced preparing this unpretentious volume, every page of which has been written under the depressive influence of intense pain, and consecrated to God in prayers and tears. These tears, prayers and purposes in all this patient labor have been like David's, who at the lowest point of his fortunes plaintively besought God, " Put Thou my tears into Thy bottle," and exclaimed in the same breath, "Thy vows are upon me, O God, I will render praises unto Thee." However imperfectly the writer may have accomplished his purpose in briefly recording the history of his life—and he feels it to have been done most inadequately—to magnify Christian patience and to praise God in the furnace of affliction have been the theme of his thoughts and the mainspring of his design. Committing this book to his family and brethren, and believing that at the gate of the kingdom of Paradise the afflictions and troubles of this life will be left behind and forgotten by those who go in and rest, he remains, in pain and patience, peace and love, faith and hope, J. H. FESPERMAN.

BARIUM SPRINGS, N. C.

INTRODUCTION.

Heroic suffering must ever command ardent admiration and call forth sublime sympathy. The iron grasp of pain, in view of no deliverance except by death, is one of life's severest ordeals. Sleepless nights that lead to the all more sleepless days, are not only the longest, but also dreariest and most depressing in all earthly existence, and when we find a "hero of faith in God," that endures all, goes through all, unmurmuringly—willing to suffer and willing to die, as it may best please or most honor God, we come to one that deserves and should receive our sincere sympathy and support. And, such a sufferer, such a hero, Pastor Fesperman is. He has learned to heed, illustrate and carry out the motto of Emperor Frederick II., that was wrung from suffering, royal, quivering lips amid the glories of a palace, when he said, "Learn to suffer patiently." Weighed down by physical ailments, cast down upon his couch by the horrors and dread effect of an unfortunate accident, he lay helpless, but not hopeless, in the humble, but neat and cosy cottage generous givers provided him with, and whilst the light of life ofttimes only flickered, he looked to and called upon God, and as in the agony of the Garden of Gethsemane, from high heaven down amid the starlight, help and strength came to Christ, so help and strength came to our brother, a "joint heir with Christ." He realized fully and often, "My grace is sufficient for thee."

In all the records of ministerial suffering in our great Lutheran Zion in America, this book of Pastor Fesperman will ever be one of the most memorable, most worthy and most deserving. Personally he enjoys the esteem of the community in which he lives and has suffered. And so has the North Carolina Synod, again and again, given expression to its kind interest in him, by deeds of love. Good people throughout the length and breadth of the land, like so many angels of mercy, have nobly come to his relief. As this has been the case, so may it be now, as he puts forth this effort and sends out this well-written and intensely interesting book from the home of his sufferings, that many all over our land will secure and use it, and learning of the sad sufferings of one of God's ministering servants, help and encourage him while life lasts, and at the same time thank God for their health, strength and unimpaired powers.

When we learn and remember that in the last two years he has lost in weight 48 pounds, we may form an idea of how intense his sufferings have been.

As the dove of Noah came to him bringing the cheering tokens of new life and new help for him, so may the book of Pastor Fesperman bring him new cheer, new help and new friends.

F. W. E. PESCHAU,

Pastor St. Paul's Evangelical Lutheran Church, and Associate Editor " The Lutheran Visitor," Wilmington, N. C.

June 18, 1892.

CHAPTER I.

I was born in Salisbury, N. C., July 7th, 1841. My parents, Cynthia and Michael Fesperman, were members of the Lutheran Church. When I was seven years old, my father, who was a mechanic, purchased a plantation in Rowan county, and I began work on the farm at a very early age. When thirteen, I was thrown from a horse, and my right leg was broken in two places. This accident occurred during the hot weather, in August, and I lay six weeks under the care of a surgeon who managed my case with such ability as to prevent lameness in after life.

The first night after I was hurt I gave myself, body and soul, to God in prayer. Although a mere boy, I had read the Bible enough to know that David's deepest repentance dared to ask, "Make me to hear joy and gladness that the bones which Thou has broken may rejoice." Young as I was, I had read and remembered that an ancient monarch, a distinguished warrior and poet, as well as an eminently holy man, once used this language, "I sought the Lord, and he heard me and delivered me from all my fears." "The angel of the Lord encampeth round about them that fear him and delivereth them." "Call upon me in the day of trouble; I will deliver thee, and thou shalt glorify me." Claiming these promises, my troubled utterances of sore need, my sighs and groans of intense suffering were accompanied by a faith which had no doubts, and which felt the beautiful summer's sun of peace, even in the mid-winter of awful pain. I have never known anything greater, wiser, better, for man to do in trouble and calamity, than to believe God's Word and trust Christ for all needed strength and guidance.

While I was confined to bed I carefully read the Bible, Book of Martyrs, Pilgrim's Progress, Alleine's Alarm, Pollock's Course of Time, and the Life of Whitfield and that of Wesley. After I was able to lay my crutches aside, I remained on the farm, but my mind constantly dwelt on the work of the ministry, and every day I knelt down and prayed the dear Lord Jesus to hear me and bless me, give me a strong mind and fluency of speech, and help me to become a worthy minister of the word. I heard the voice of the Lord, saying: "Whom shall I send, and who will go for us? Then said I, Here am I: send me."

"I have neither gold nor silver,
  But my life I freely give;
I can point men to the Saviour,
  I can tell them, look and live!
Weak am I; but Thou art mighty,
  And Thy strength my strength shall be;
Master, hear me,—take me,—use me,—
  Here am I, send even me."
" Anywhere let me announce Thy sweet name;
  Anywhere speak of Thy cross and Thy shame;
Anywhere let me Thy great love declare,—
  Oh, let me work for Thee, Lord, anywhere."

When my father died, I was left poor and helpless; but wiping the tears from my eyes, I exclaimed, "My Father in heaven, I look to Thee and sue for Thy protection and tenderness, and humbly pray that the heart of my widowed mother may be comforted and that my precious Saviour may permit her to survive to hear me preach His gospel." When my mother complained of being sick, I always ran into the room and, falling on my knees by the side of the loom where she wove, I prayed for her life, promising the Lord that if He would spare her, I would in return for His mercy try to be a faithful preacher of righteousness. God answered my prayers, permitted her to hear me preach, and prolonged her life to seventy-three years.

I had no opportunity to attend school, but I read many books by fire-light and acquired much correct and useful knowledge by listening to the conversation of well-informed men. I made it a rule, when I went into the society of educated people, to be quiet and attentive, and I always had new knowledge to think about when I returned to my home and work. I owe much to silence and close observation. I read a large number and a great variety of interesting books; and when there was uncertainty concerning the pronunciation of a word I charged my memory with it and watched until some educated minister, well trained teacher or accomplished public speaker uttered it. Thus I learned to pronounce hundreds of words. Knowing that little upon little, line upon line, is the law of progress and achievement, I endeavored to observe this law carefully, faithfully, patiently, unwaveringly, doing the best I could in whatever circumstances I was placed, and at the same time directing all the powers of mind and body toward the desired object,—preaching.

I was fond of history, loved to attend debating societies, and took great interest in reading the *New York Ledger*, and much pride in relating its stories to people about me. I studied some theological books, and my desire to preach became intensified. I retired to bed thinking about preaching, I dreamed of it, talked in my sleep concerning it, and when I awoke it was the first thought to enter my mind. This ardent desire to preach was not created by a revival of religion, or produced by any impression made on my mind in the house of God, or originated by any person speaking to me concerning the ministry, but was on my mind when, on my knees, I prayed, "Dear Lord Jesus Christ, spare the life of my precious mother and I will try to preach Thy Word." I could not refrain from preaching. The boys of the neighborhood erected for me a pulpit, with steps attached and a book-board on it, and I preached to them in the woods almost every Sunday noon. This was not child's play. We had our Bibles and Hymn Books, and we sang, prayed and behaved ourselves. Some aged men and their families attended our services and encouraged me in my efforts, but there was no one able to furnish money to educate me. A retrospect of my whole life, from the earliest period of my recollection down to the present hour, leaves me with this impression, that I have been and am being guided by a gracious and mighty Hand, which has made and is making that possible to me which otherwise to me had been impossible. The adverse circumstances by which I was surrounded in early life all indicated the impossibility of preparing myself for the ministry. God gave me a retentive mind, tenacity of purpose, something to do, something to love, something to hope for, and inspired me with heroic aspirations and resolutions which enabled me to overcome many difficulties.

I was invited sometimes to speak in Methodist churches, and at camp meetings, where I had abundant opportunity for the exercise of mind and tongue. I went in company with Rev. W. Kimball, a worthy Lutheran minister, to attend a church where the pastor, Rev. J. A. Linn, was conducting a series of meetings. After being present several days I was requested by the pastor to preach the morning sermon. I asked to be excused, saying "I am not a preacher," but he persisted in his request and replied, "I will be responsible; go into the pulpit and preach." He accompanied me to the pulpit, I entered it and after preliminary services I announced these words as my text, "I must work the works of Him that sent me while it is day; the night cometh when no man can work." While I was in the midst of my discourse some aged men and women commenced clapping their hands and shouting, and one young man ran into the pulpit praising God. The pastor of this congregation was my friend in all his after years, and in his death his good wife lost a kind husband, his children an affectionate father and the Lutheran church an efficient and pious pastor. Often and often in after years I have turned by happy habit to feel his beautiful friendship at hand, only to remember with a fresh touch of sadness that God took from me that presence so kind and so dear. Yet, from the very bottom of my heart I give thanks to the Lord and Saviour, who has him in keeping, that it was my honor and my joy to know and to love Rev. J. A. Linn.

CHAPTER II.

I was invited by Methodist and other ministers to conduct services and deliver addresses in their churches, and many professed Christ in these meetings, but some people said, "This boy frightens his hearers, makes them shout and faint, and he has no license to do this." Those were days when revivals prevailed in the church. There were no evangelists. Faithful and laborious pastors generally held a series of meetings in their churches, which sometimes continued from one to two weeks. These solemn assemblies, led by their pastor, prayed to God for an outpouring of His Spirit, and frequently people came to the "anxious seat" and professed religion. Those were also days when members of the church expected their pastors, not strangers, to instruct and lead them in the way of salvation, and every reputable pastor was required to hold license or ordination papers.

Already in childhood I carefully searched the Scriptures; there never was a moment when I doubted a promise in God's word, and my desire to preach did not come by a miracle or through a vision, but it was on my mind and heart from childhood. I owe my desire to be a minister, to God and not to men. My prayer was "O Lord God of my life, Thou whom I worshipped at my mother's knee, and to whom my heart goes up in trust and confidence, accept my life—my hands, my feet, my voice, my lips, my intellect, my will, my heart, my love, all that I am—and let them be consecrated to thee." I had no pecuniary means with which to educate myself, but studied with all my faculties. concentrated on one object—entrance into the regular ministry of the church.

When the war between the north and south was precipitated and entrance into the army became unavoidable, I packed Schmucker's Popular Theology, Gregory's Evidences of Christianity, Porter's Homiletics, the Lives of the Ancient Philosophers. my Bible and Hymn Book into my knapsack, and went into the service of the Confederacy against all my inclinations, but thank God my mind was not warped by prejudice, and my heart was not debased by ill will. I recognized a brother in every country and Christians. in every church. I endured many deprivations in the army, but I was not guilty of taking any article of food or clothing. I refused to eat stolen rations. License or no license, I intended to preach, and many times exercised the talents I possessed in exhorting the soldiers to become Christ's followers, and live consistent and blameless lives. Some preferred cards to these services, but not a few gave me their cards to burn and manifested a disposition to join me in praying for their salvation.

When we were in camp or in winter quarters I gave my whole time to theological studies. Rev. L. A. Bikle, who had been a professor of ancient languages in North Carolina College, was chaplain of the 20th regiment in my brigade. This dear brother, an influential member of the Evangelical Lutheran Synod of North Carolina, was a friend of mine before the war commenced; and when I was in the army, if I did not comprehend a point in theology, or did not know the correct pronunciation of a word, I managed to get into his company, inquired about what I desired to know and charged my memory with his opinions. In this way I obtained much important and useful information. I lost my books several times, but secured others and continued to pursue my studies, enduring all the hardships of a soldier's life until I was captured in battle at Chancellorsville, and taken to Clifton Barracks, Washington, D. C. Here I preached the night after my arrival. While I was adressing the prisoners I was somewhat startled by the appearance of two gentlemen, who, with their hats in their hands, advanced through the department to where I was speaking, and sat down as attentive hearers. After the service closed, one of the gentlemen took me by the hand, saying,

"My name is Colonel Alexander, I am the commander of these Barracks, and I will provide better quarters and fare for you: I do not think you ought to be among these rough, hard men." He then introduced me to his Lieutenant-Colonel, and immediately called for Sergeant Halliday, of New York, ordered him to provide good fare and quarters for me, and instructed him to allow me the privilege of taking walks outside the prison walls. In these walks I occasionally met Colonel Alexander, and many times lucrative railroad positions and superior educational facilities were offered to me: on terms, however, that I could not conscientiously accept.

Doubtless at this period of my life my love for my mother and my home helped to lay my entire future on the altar of terrible misfortune—helped to destroy the incomprehensible and nameless something that was then endeavouring to lay at my feet the precious, golden sceptre of success. "Everybody," the old proverb says, "has his day:" and so every human being has at least his one opportunity. "There is a deep nick in time's restless wheel for each man's foot." I now believe that the whole of my future destiny in regard to earthly prosperity depended on the decision I made when the Commander of Clifton Barracks, to induce me to take the oath of allegiance, offered me a lucrative position, under the written signature of the President of the United States. This was the crisis of my life; everything was then concentrated on a single point. The whole of our lives often depend on some single action that shall determine the character, and that shall send an influence ever onward. A right or wrong decision then settles everything. The moment, when in the battle at Waterloo, the Duke of Wellington could say, "This will do," decided the fate of battle, and of kingdoms. A wrong movement just at that point might have changed the condition of the world for centuries. In every man's life there are such periods; and probably in the lives of most men their future course is more certainly determined by one such far-reaching decision than by many actions in other circumstances. There are moments when honor, wealth, usefulness, health and salvation seem all to depend on a single resolution. My destiny, in regard to pecuniary advantages and educational facilities, was settled adversely by a single decision in prison, when pure love for my mother, outweighing all other considerations, constrained me to return home. In sickness and in sorrow, in captivity, in any and all circumstances, my heart invariably turned to my mother and home.

"A mother's care, how sweet the name;
What is a mother's love?
A noble, pure and tender flame
Enkindled from above:
To bless a heart of earthly mould,
The warmest love that can't grow cold.
This is a mother's love."

After several months of prison life in Washington city, I was exchanged, came home and then returned to the 5th North Carolina Regiment, and, on account of general debility, was detailed as a clerk in a Confederate States' Arsenal, located in Salisbury, N. C. I had no connection with a prison there. While in Salisbury I again began gathering books until I had secured a nice library of interesting works. But these precious treasures were not to last long. Part of a Division of United States soldiers, under the command of General Stoneman, came through the country, set fire to the Arsenal, the flames reached my room and consumed books, clothing, and all I possessed. I was taken a prisoner and conveyed on foot through the mountains of North Carolina to Tennessee, and from thence by railroad to Camp Chase, Ohio, where I suffered many great privations until several months after the war closed. There were twelve ministers confined in Camp Chase, and we held interesting services every Sunday. I prayed for the prisoners and preached to them, but my heart yearned for my home and for proper authority to declare God's Word. I came from prison to my mother's home at length, sick and penniless, and found myself in the midst of a face to face, hand to hand, inch by inch, conflict with unfortunate circumstances, and I was not allowed to choose my foes, my battle-fields, my ammunition or my generals. It was very plain that if I entered the ministry I must fight and my battles could not be conducted on any prearranged plan. My conflicts had to be single handed skirmishes with "ugly guerrillas" that came down upon me in the "shape and guise" of poverty and need on all sides, and a few personal enemies resembling hooded snakes in canebrakes. In all difficulties, trials, needs, and in the presence of a few envious enemies, things that seemed to indicate the impossibility of my entrance into the ministry, I found comfort in praying and in reading this passage of Scripture: "And I will make thee unto this people a fenced and brazen wall; and they shall fight against thee, but they shall not prevail against thee, for I am with thee to save thee, and to deliver thee, saith the Lord." Reading this assurance and believing that whether poor or rich, distinguished or obscure, whether in the city or lonely spreading waste, He who is rich in the brilliant glory of a thousand suns, is true to His promises and to His people, I became oblivious to external circumstances. I continued my studies with indomitable resolution, with sleepless energy, with tireless tenacity of purpose, saying to evil example around me, to the need of a better education confronting me, to poverty and need ever present with me, and to the sneer of anticipated derision, " Here I stand, determined to preach, I can do naught else, God help me. Amen." And God, whose power made the lilies bloom and sent the ravens, as ministers of mercy, to bring his prophet bread--whose love shall kindle its brilliant suns when other lights have gone out—whose tender mercy will sing its beautiful songs while the trumpet of the archangel peals and the air is filled with the crash of breaking sepulchres, and the rush of the wings of the rising dead, heard my prayers and helped me. It is an historical fact that prayer walks in safety down the centuries by the side of unexpected disclosures of the world's improvement, and that its wonderful power has been vindicated from hostile criticism by the experience of all generations. May each reader of this book "pray much; God loves a sweet, dependent spirit that owns itself too weak to walk alone. No prayer is uttered but listening angels hear it, sometimes in ways mysterious and unknown. Their answers come; but surely as the light hears the dawn calling and dispels the night, so do those blessed messengers on high hear and bless us when we cry." The history of the prayers of the past may be put into one sentence: "They looked unto Him and were lightened, and their faces were not ashamed," and as for the present I thank God that I can say "This poor man cried, and the Lord heard him and saved him out of all his troubles." I prayed for sympathy and God answered me. Revs. W. Kimball and Simeon Scherer lent me books and I committed to memory volumes of interesting works, including the "Formula for the Government and Discipline of the Evangelical Lutheran Church." I was determined to undergo a creditable examination when I applied for license to preach, and I spent whole nights without sleep in reading my books and praying. I remembered how the prophet's servant climbed the steeps of Carmel to look for the first signal of God's mercy. Three years, and never a cloud dappled the burning sky. Three long years, and never a dewdrop had glistened on the grass or kissed the lips of a dying flower, and for the need of rain, famine, desolation, and death reigned everywhere. But the cloud in answer to importunate prayer came at last. No larger than a man's hand, it rose from the sea; it spread: and as he saw the first lightning's flash, and heard the first thunder's roll, he forgot all his toils, and would have climbed the hills, not seven times, but seventy times seven, to hail that welcome sight. Just so it was with me; I considered the ministry worth praying for, toiling for, suffering for, and after years of struggles God crowned my efforts with success. Revs. W. Kimball, L. C. Groseclose, Simeon Scherer and J. Crim, advised me to apply for license to enter upon the work of the ministry, and furnished me with letters commending me to the favorable notice of the officers of the Evangelical Lutheran Synod of North Carolina.

On the 7th of December, 1865, I was carefully examined and received *ad-interim* license from Rev. J. B. Anthony, President of the North Carolina Synod. I hastened from Mt. Pleasant, N. C., where I was examined, a distance of eighteen miles, to my home in Rowan county, where I told my mother the joyful news that I held in my possession the longed for credentials to declare the Word of God. Without delay and without synodical aid, I took charge of a mission field consisting of two churches in Davie Co., North Carolina, where I labored until 1869, when constant chills and the need of increased salary compelled me to resign my work. I immediately moved to a healthy section in Rowan Co., and commenced preaching twice every Sunday in a school house, where after much suffering and hard labor I organized a congregation of forty members, and erected a house of worship, which we had good reasons to name " Providence." By taking this organization into connection with the Iredell charge I managed to serve it ten years.

On the 19th of September, 1866, I married Miss C. A. Lentz, whose true heart has never faltered, and whose footsteps have never wearied in the pathway of love for twenty and five years.

I was called to St. Paul's Church in Iredell Co., in 1869, and to St. Michael's, in the same county, in 1871, and resigned the entire charge in 1878. While I was pastor of the congregations in Iredell, I supplied Thyatira and Beth Eden churches in Catawba county with preaching. During a number of years I preached to six congregations.

These churches, located in three counties, made my field of labor a very trying one to serve. In order to be faithful in the discharge of my duties to my family and to the Church, I was frequently compelled to travel on the railroad and on foot all hours of the night, and this exposure, in the course of time, ruined my constitution. Love for home and family has been a ruling power in my life. I often preached twice on Sunday and walked twenty-five miles through the darkness of night, reaching my wife and children by daylight next morning. I never left my home without telling my wife where I could be found each night of my absence, and when she might confidently expect my return, and in all my ministry she was never once disappointed in the arrangements. My greatest happiness was always found in the society of my wife and children. I kept a large blank book in which I frequently wrote letters containing affectionate parental advice to each member of my family.

> " Father, my wife and children!
> I know not what is coming on the earth;
> Beneath the shadow of Thy heavenly wing,
> Oh, keep them, keep them, Thou who gavest them birth;
> Oh, keep them undefiled!
> Unspotted from a tempting world of sin;
> That, clothed in white, through the bright city gates
> They may with me in triumph enter in."

The minutes of the Ministerium of the North Carolina Synod show that a favorable vote for my ordination was cast at Pilgrim Church, Davidson Co., North Carolina, August the 26th, 1871, but the vow was not assumed, or the laying on of hands, or prayer given, until in October of the same year.

CHAPTER III.

I suffered many years with disease of the lungs and heart before I resigned my pastoral work in Iredell and Catawba counties.

I frequently preached with large blister plasters over the region of both lungs, and my whole chest was completely scarred by the constant use of blistering ointment, Croton oil and other irritants. I labored in the pulpit more than one hundred and sixty times with sores produced by blisters larger than silver dollars, on each breast. I often went into God's altar suffering, with a psalm in my mouth, and thus glorified my precious Saviour in the midst of the fires of affliction. Eternity alone can reveal how much I endured for Christ's sake before I relinquished the active work of the ministry. The Scriptures assure me that every minister of Jesus Christ is a watchman on Zion, and the poet paints his relations well, and pencils his duty and danger with the hand of a master, when, with the watchman in his eye, and on the eve of a conflict with the powers of darkness, he exclaims:

"In heaven's high arch above his head, a glorious form appeared,
Whose left hand bore a flambeau light, his right a scepter reared;
A diadem of purest gold his brow imperial crowned,
And from his throne he thus addressed the watchman on his round:
What of the night, what of the night? Watchman; What of the night?
The myriad foe, in close array, come on to try their might—
A night assault—and if thy trump mistake a single sound,
I'll hang upon these battlements, the watchman on his round."

Even the most faithful watchmen, those of rarest worth, may fall in the conflict, but, it will be from the walls of Zion, or upon the hill of God, and they sink in death, with the world for their shrine and mankind their mourners. A minister of Jesus Christ is God's mouth-piece to man. He is to guard and dispense, with the most sacred and uncompromising jealousy, the heavenly treasures of wisdom and knowledge, committed to him in trust for the reformation of his kind. Amid all the pleasures of my life there is one that is finer than all, and amid all the joys that bloomed in the landscape of my days, there is one whose flower stands preëminent, whose beauty is enjoyed to-day, and whose fragrance fills the atmosphere of my suffering life with delight. It is the pleasure and joy of knowing I have led sinners to repentance. I knew and felt the responsibility of being a mouth-piece for God, a minister for Jesus Christ, and labored for the Saviour as long as my poor suffering body would allow me. When I could no longer stand as a watching sentinel upon the walls of the Church, I cast my burden upon my precious Saviour, saying: "Dear Lord Jesus, I am too feeble to watch longer, but the seed is sown, the bread is cast upon the waters, and if I have improved a single soul, given birth to any pious purposes, dried up any tears, checked any sighs, bound up any broken hearts, or poured the balsam of hope and the balm of life into any wounded spirits, then I have not watched and prayed, and lived and labored in vain.

> Though sickness now holds me in a chain,
>   No will can break or bend to earthly use,
> I can still pray and truthfully exclaim :
>
> "In the cross of Christ I glory,
> Towering over the wreck of time ;
>   All the light of sacred story
> Gathers round its head sublime.
>
> "When the woes of life overtake me,
>   Hope deceives and pains annoy,
> Never shall the cross forsake me ;
>   Lo! it glows with peace and joy,
>
> Bane and blessing, pain and pleasure,
>   By the cross are sanctified ;
> Peace is there that knows no measure,
>   Joys that through all time abide."
>
> "In the cross of Christ I glory."

In the year 1879 the condition of my health rendered it absolutely necessary for me to retire from the active work of the ministry. Trusting that I might recuperate, I rested a short time, but my expectations were disappointed. I gradually grew weaker and worse. Having a wife and seven children to support, I was in an unenviable condition, but I had already experienced the mercy and faithfulness of God in too many severe trials ever to waver in my trust and confidence in Him whose hand is not shortened that it can not save, and whose grace is not limited. I remembered these touching and assuring words, which are sufficient to make weak faith ashamed:

"Commit thou all thy griefs,
   And ways into His hands,
To His sure truth and tender care,
   Who earth and heaven commands;
Who points the clouds their course,
   Whom winds and seas obey,
He shall direct thy wandering feet,
   He shall *prepare* thy way.
God can this hour with every dainty
   The poor man's table amply spread,
And strip the rich of all his plenty,
   And send him forth to beg his bread.
Sing, pray and in God's ways walk ever,
   And all your duties well perform;
Distrust Him for His blessing never,
   And he will shield you from all harm,
For he who in the Lord confides,
   Upon a solid rock abides."

I was not able to preach and had no way to provide for my family, but just before stern want would have approached our door, Eugene B. Drake, editor of the Statesville *American*, an aged and respected member of the Episcopal church, and one of the purest hearted men I ever knew, employed me to keep the books and to manage the affairs of a commercial establishment, which, on account of the death of a partner, was then going out of business. My connection with Father Drake was exceedingly pleasant. Nothing could exceed his kindness toward me while I was in his employment, and there was that in him that made an impression upon my memory that promises to stand well the test of time. In all my association with Mr. Drake we did not have a single difference, and he tried to make my life pleasant. In September, 1879, I was invited by the Council of Bethel Church, Stanly county, to hold a communion service for their congregation. Sick and weak as I was, I accepted the invitation, taking my family to Salisbury, where some of the Council met us with vehicles and conveyed us to their hospitable homes in the neighborhood of the house of God. We remained with the people two weeks. I preached five times, administered the communion, baptized several children and confirmed several persons. The last day of my services at Bethel, the Council of the church proposed to give me a call and requested me to consent to become their pastor, but knowing that my extreme feebleness precluded hope of ability to serve them, I refused to allow my name to be proposed in a congregational meeting. A few weeks after my return to Statesville I received several kind and interesting letters again asking me to give my consent to become the pastor of Bethel congregation, to which I replied that it would be imprudent for me to allow myself to be called to serve a people when I was conscious of the fact that I would fall and die in their midst. They immediately wrote that if I fell while on duty and died in their midst I would certainly do so among my sincere friends. Having seven small children to provide for, no money and no way to support my family, and being satisfied that the people in Stanly were warm-hearted friends, I answered, saying, that they might arrange for me a temporary parsonage at Misenheimer's Sulphur Springs, bring wagons, meet me in Salisbury, and convey me to their community. Their response to this proposal was hearty and prompt, and in November, 1879, we moved to Stanly county, where I was destined to become thoroughly disabled. Soon after my arrival in Stanly, I held a series of meetings in Bethel Church, in which I was assisted by the members, many of whom were earnest, praying men. I could ask almost any member of this church to pray in public, knowing that he would respond. I preached to St. Stephen's Church several times, and once to a struggling congregation in Gold Hill, but was too feeble to take charge of these churches. I desire to leave on record that Dr. Shimpoch, a successful physician, and zealous member of the congregation in Gold Hill, did much to cheer and assist me in the work I had attempted to do in his church. This faithful physician and his Christian wife, deserve and have my grateful remembrance. Dr. Shimpoch knew my physical condition, but he did all he could to inspire me with hope. I continued to preach at Bethel Church until I could scarcely read a verse in the Bible or hymn book without making repeated efforts to get a full inspiration of breath, and even until I no longer had the strength necessary to stand in the pulpit. When I sat down, it took much effort to rise without assistance, and in this wretched condition I leaned on the "book board" and addressed my hearers. At last extreme debility, accompanied by chilly sensations and hectic fevers, confined me to bed, where I had exhausting night sweats, coughed incessantly, and frequently when I expanded my chest the pus from my diseased lung gushed from my mouth. Excessive coughing and great difficulty in breathing made it necessary for me to occupy a sitting posture in bed,

"Where I had such long weakness
 And such wearing pain,
As had no end in view, that made my life
 One weary avenue of darkened days,
The bitter darkness growing darker still,
 Which none could share or soothe, which sundered me
From all desire, or hope, or strife of change,
 Or service of my Master in the world,
Or fellowship with all the faces round
 Of passing pains and pleasures,—while my pain
Passed not,—and only this
 Remained for me to look for,—more pain,
And doubt if I could bear it to the end."

My wife and friends watched by my bed day and night, only to see me sink lower and lower, until my feet touched the earth at the very brink of the grave, but at that point the Almighty power of God was waiting to arrest my descent into the dark chambers of the dead. As in all cases of lung disease, my understanding was unimpaired—my mind was perfectly bright, and I was permitted to bear testimony before my surrounding friends to the unspeakable consolations of the Holy Spirit, to the unfailing faithfulness of God, and to the abundant love of the Redeemer. Practicing physicians from different sections visited me professionally and pronounced my condition beyond the reach of medical skill. One of the medical men examined me and then pronounced his opinion thus: "Mr. Fesperman, your left lung is about gone and your right lung is seriously involved, and you cannot hope to get well." My answer to this candid physician was this, "I am not afraid to die, for death himself shall some day expire and the giant corpse of time lie buried in the grave of years, when I have just commenced to sing the beautiful songs of my precious Saviour; but I have a wife and seven helpless children, and for their sake I shall try to live, greeting life as God may give it and yet awaiting death when He shall send it." The doctor smiled and remarked, "Your resolution is a strong and good one, but your case is just as I have informed you." Every hope of my recovery seemed to vanish from the minds of my family and friends; for all the physicians, some of whom were skilled in their profession, had said that my death was not in the distant future. There is no death to those who know of life. No time to those who see eternity. I looked at my dependent wife and children and felt that I was encompassed with grief on every side, but still the flower of love and trust bloomed on, enabling me to exclaim, "O Lord, my strength, and fortress, and refuge, in this day of affliction and trouble," while the waves of sorrow threaten

"Me and mine to swallow up,
  Troubles fall and trials thicken,
Cry I, while I drain the cup,
  Thou Lord art my hiding place.
In the secret of His presence
  The Lord keeps I know not how;
In the shadow of the Highest
  I am *resting, hiding, now.*"

In such moments of sorrowful visitation from the living God, we may show that fortitude with which human nature often breasts the storms of calamity; but there can be no holy submission, no perfect resignation, no absolute peace, except to those to whom the voice of faith can whisper, "The eternal God is thy refuge, and underneath are the everlasting arms."

One beautiful Sunday morning Mrs. Julia Misenheimer, who visited me several times every day, came to my bedside and endeavored to encourage me. After conversing with me a short time she walked to the door, turned, and looking at me remarked, "Brother Fesperman, if you die you will have to expire under the tears and earnest prayers of your people, for we all meet in the church this morning to pray for your life—to ask the Lord to spare you to your family and to the Church." The house of God that day became the scene of solemn, tearful wrestlings with the Angel of the Covenant, that yet a little while I might be spared. Faith, hope,—pleading faith, humble hope,—were there in Bethel Church; and almost awed to silence, but laboring all the more intensely, from the very pressure under which they bent, and seeming to say, "Lord, we cannot give this sick pastor up. Oh! let this husband, father and minister of Thy Word live."

May God bless the members of Bethel Church; they were true to me and true to my wife and children. They abundantly provided the comforts of life for my family while I lay sick in their midst. Bro. Claiborn Misenheimer, who owned a mill near by, came every day to inquire concerning my welfare. One morning as he stood at the foot of my bed, I noticed him shedding tears. He said: "Brother Fesperman, if I can do anything in the world for you—if you desire anything, tell me what it is, and if money can secure it, you shall have it." I answered that I wished to use a certain remedy that I had read about in the *Lutheran Observer*, but that the price of it was exceedingly high. He inquired what it cost, and in half an hour Mrs. Mary Misenheimer stood by my bed with the money in her hand. A letter was quickly written, and in one week the medicine reached me, and, as I believe, in answer to my prayer proved beneficial. Infidelity may smile at this assertion, but it is certainly evident that the efficacy of prayer was plainly manifested when my case was given up as hopeless by the ablest physicians—when all who knew my condition thought it not possible for me to survive a week longer. The united prayers not only of my own church, but of Christians of other denominations, went up to the mercy-seat in my behalf, and the hand of the destroyer was stayed. The Lord's people unitedly prayed for my life, and although I was not healed, the progress of my disease was arrested in its rapid, destructive course, and my days were mercifully prolonged.

"God's eye is fixed on seraph throngs;
   His arm upholds the sky;
His ear is filled with angel songs,
   His love is throned on high.
The sun and moon and twinkling stars,
   And lightning chariots swift that fly,
And all the flowers that bloom on earth
   Would fade without the love of that all-shining Eye.
Each tiny thing within, without,
   Beneath our feet, or in the sky,
Or mighty men who rule the land,
   Live in the love and light of that great Eye.
The vapors from the boundless sea,
   The mists that on the mountains lie,
And clouds that veil the starry sky,
   All float in that all-seeing Eye.
No warbled note, nor placid smile,
   No joyous shout, nor parting sigh
But wends its way from things that die,
   To live in that all-loving Eye.
There is a power which helpless man can wield,
   When mortal aid is vain,
That eye, that arm, that love to reach,
   That listening ear to gain.
That power is prayer, which soars on high,
   Through Jesus, to the throne;
And moves the hand which moves the world
   To bring our blessings down."

In the month of April, 1880, my wife, and sister Misenheimer, holding me by the arms, led me out of the house into the beautiful sunshine that I might enjoy a sun-bath. My people told the doctors that if there was any hope of my ever being able to preach for them again, they would not call a pastor but wait a year or more, and in the intervening time provide the comforts of life for my family. The medical gentlemen promptly and candidly informed my generous friends and beloved parishioners that I was afflicted with consumption in an advanced stage, associated with heart disease; that it was possible for me to live a while, but that I would never get well. The kind proposal of my friends at Bethel to provide for my family and wait for preaching until I recovered, brought to my mind this kind of verse:

> "The world is full of good advice,
>   Of prayers and praise and preaching nice;
>   But generous souls resembling these who aid mankind
>   Are like to diamonds—hard to find.
>   Give like a Christian—speak in deeds;
>   A noble life's the best of creeds,
>   And he shall wear a royal crown
>   Who gives a lift when men are down."

In May, 1880, the North Carolina Synod held its annual meeting in Mt. Pleasant, not far from me. Anxious to see my brethren, I had myself conveyed to the synod, but was too weak to attend its sessions. I was obliged to retire to a private house, where I remained during the day, and then returned home completely exhausted. My ministerial brethren sent me a donation by the hands of Marvel Ritchie, who was the delegate from Bethel congregation. Shortly after the meeting of synod, I concluded to return to Iredell county, a higher and healthier locality. Bethel Church being close to my residence, I caused an announcement to be made that I would hold a Silent Communion there, and bid adieu to my congregation. At the the appointed time we assembled in the church and the congregation sang these words :

> "Our souls by love together knit,
> Cemented, mixed in one,
> One hope, one heart, one mind, one voice,
> 'Tis heaven on earth begun."

One of the Council prayed. I then consecrated the bread and wine, and silently administered to the communicants. This was indeed a solemn scene, and many tears were shed during the services. One aged lady, now in heaven, where robes, and palms, and crowns, and harpings feebly denote celestial triumphs, stood at the communion table, and as I approched her with the elements of the Lord's Supper in my hand, gave expression to her feelings by glorifying and praising God.

The day arrived for my departure from Stanly county. The people gave me forty dollars and two sacks of flour to take with me to my home in Statesville, N. C.

The wagons were loaded ready to move, and the members came to say good-by, when one of the officers of the church, whose body now slumbers in the repose of death and whose spirit doubtless lives in the glory of his Father's house, took me by the hand, saying, "Bro. Fesperman, what is your parting advice to us?" I replied, "Love and trust your Saviour. Look to Him by repentance, by faith and in the faithful performance of every Christian duty. Read your Bible. Learn here the science of salvation, unfolded in lines of light. This will point your spirits to the only healing Hand that pours the balm of eternal life into the souls of men, and will turn your sight undaunted on the tomb. Forget not that prayer is man in humble, earnest negotiation with his God; that it is the moral nerve quickening the muscles of the soul to approach the Almighty, and that if your prayers go to heaven, laden with sighs and stained with tears, they shall return accompanied by angels and freighted with blessings. —Farewell."

As the wagons conveyed me away from the scene of my sufferings, and from the hearts of my faithful Christian friends, I could truly appreciate these lines:

> "Blest be the tie that binds
> Our hearts in Christian love!
> The fellowship of kindred minds
> Is like to that above.
> We share our mutual woes,
> Our mutual burdens bear;
> And often for each other flows
> The sympathizing tear.
> When we asunder part,
> It gives us inward pain;
> But we shall still be joined in heart
> And hope to meet again."

This last verse expresses the feelings that accompanied me when I left my friends and parishioners in Stanly county. When we reached our former home in Iredell county, I was so feeble that I could scarcely walk one hundred yards. It was evident that the great sea of disease was gradually eating away the bank and shoal of time upon which I existed. Here I learned by sore affliction that it was a loving Providence that made man's earthly home so little fit for him, that he might seek the city which hath foundations — the beautiful city with its God-built stories—its rainbow coverings and sun-like splendors—crowded with the redeemed, and the Lord in the midst to chase the winter of affliction away.

We had seven children, all of whom were too small to do anything by which to feed and clothe themselves, and having spent all except fifty cents of the money given to us by former parishioners, we knew that some prompt action was necessary to keep want from coming to our door. To trust God when our houses and bags are full, and our tables are spread, is no hard thing; but to trust Him when our purses are empty, but a handful of meal and a cruse of oil left, and all the ways of relief stopped— herein lies the measure of a Christian's grace. Nearly all our money was spent and we had no prospect of any relief. In this extremity we committed our cause to God in earnest prayer, truly believing that anything would be possible rather than that the most tremulous trust in the Lord Jesus Christ should go unblest and unanswered. We trusted in the Lord and encouraged our hearts to hope in His mercy and faithfulness. Our afflictions were many and sore, and our present circumstances embarrassing, and our prospects for the future exceedingly gloomy. Providence seemed to have set us up as a mark for the arrows of adversity. Stroke upon stroke had been experienced. Billow after billow had gone over us, but we did not give way to despondency and unprofitable repining at the course of events. Considering ourselves under the safe conduct of Almighty God, and knowing that He who is the Lord of time will ever save at the best possible moments, our faith enabled us to sing these beautiful, heart cheering verses:

> "It may not be *my* way,
> It may not be *thy* way,
> And yet in His *own* way
> The *Lord* will provide.
> It may not be *my* time,
> It may not be *thy* time,
> And yet in *His own* time
> The *Lord* will provide."

He did not provide so quickly as to prevent us from feeling our need, neither did He tarry so long as to make us sick with hope deferred, or so long as to permit unfortunate circumstances to bring us to absolute want. The next day, He rebuked our fear and rewarded our faith. For while we were conjecturing where the needed aid was to come from, a team, attached to a wagon, halted at our gate, and a small lad got out of the vehicle, entered the yard, advanced to the door, and said, "I am from Catawba county; my name is Robert Yount; you baptized my sisters." I immediately recognized him to be the son of the talented physician, Dr. McD. Yount, whom I considered the most liberal man I had ever met, under whom I had read medicine, whose children I had baptized, and with whom I had spent some of the happiest social hours of my life. Little Robert remarked, "Father heard that you were sick and he has sent you some flour, potatoes, and other things. He then handed me a match box, and when I entered the house and opened it, I found seventy five cents and these words written on a scrap of paper. " Please accept this gift from three little children whom you baptized."

I then thanked God and in gratitude exclaimed:

> " Though waves and storms go o'er my head,
> Though health and strength be gone,
> Though joys be withered all and dead :
> Though every comfort be withdrawn.
> On this my steadfast soul relies,
> The dear Lord Jesus never dies."

When the donation from Dr. Yount was almost expended, a colored man, who then waited on Mrs. Vernem, an aged Christian lady from New York, but who is now the pastor of a large and wealthy congregation of colored people in New Jersey, came to my door, handed me a letter and immediately retired. I opened the envelope and found five dollars, and these encouraging words : " My dear Christian friends, please accept this small token of my love and esteem, accompanied by my sincere prayers to God in your behalf." This God-sent gift came just in time to relieve great mental solicitude.

Soon after this, Dr. C. A. Stork, a lovable Lutheran pastor in Baltimore, Md., who since then has cast his throbbing dust aside, to put his diadem of deathless glory on, sent me five dollars, accompanied by his prayers and sincere sympathy. The tender spirit manifested in his letter made me feel that he was indeed a true brother, worthy of contact with the throne and palace of God, the river and tree of life, the family and pavilion, the splendor and equipage of heaven, in full and satisfying fruition. I have lived and struggled with sufferings, but Dr. Stork was taken in the prime of full manhood to dwell where

> "No blasted flower,
> Or withered bud celestial gardens know:
> No scorching blast or fierce, descending shower
> Scatters destruction like a ruthless foe."

When I was in the greatest need of pecuniary assistance, Thomas A. Scott, who was Secretary of War during the administration of President Lincoln, and afterward president of the Pennsylvania railroad, wrote me a touching letter and transmitted to me his check for one hundred dollars. This generous donor was then at White Sulphur Springs, Va., sick with Bright's disease, and he died the year following and doubtless is now where

> "No battle word
> Startles the sacred host with fear and dread,
> The song of peace creation's morning heard,
> Is sung wherever angels tread."

I was confined to my bed almost the whole of my time by weakness and pain, but believing that the soul which cries aloud to God, the God and Father of our Lord Jesus Christ, though it have no language but a cry, would never call in vain, I prayed very sincerely that Almighty God would open the way for me to secure a farm for a permanent home for my wife and children. With a burdened mind conscious of its great need of heavenly support I rolled my burden of cares and needs upon the arm of Jehovah. "I sought the Lord and He heard me, and delivered me from all my fears." In the latter part of November, 1880, I received a letter from Mrs. M. D. Harter, of Mansfield, Ohio, in which she said: "Enclosed you will find three drafts, each of five dollars, on New York. It is a shame that any minister in our church should be in need." This communication reached me late in the night, and I did not close my eyes in sleep until I had addressed the kind donor a suitable acknowledgment, in the latter part of which I mentioned my anxiety concerning the future of my family. In a few days I received a letter from her husband, Mr. M. D. Harter, telling me that he had read the acknowledgment I had addressed to his wife, that it touched his heart, that I should look for a farm, and that he would interest himself in my behalf and contribute to secure it for my family.

This was an answer to my prayers, but I was too sick to travel over the country in search of lands for sale, and there was no trustworthy, intelligent person in the community whom I could ask to attend to my business. By diligent inquiry, however, we heard of a small farm which could be purchased for six hundred and fifty dollars. I immediately communicated the news to my friend, Mr. M. D. Harter, but before the money to pay for it reached me the proprietor sold it to another individual, and we could not learn of a plantation in Iredell county with open land and buildings on it that could be bought for less than fifteen or eighteen hundred dollars. At last we heard of a body of woodland for sale which was said to have some open ground but no buildings on it. Sick near unto death and exceedingly anxious to locate my family, and being fully aware of the impossibility of doing any better with the amount of money promised, I traded for it, but was deceived, for the place did not have an acre of cleared land or a building of any kind on it. At this time my physicians and myself believed that I could not survive until the plantation was secured. I wrote this opinion to Rev. H. C. Haithcox, of Muncy, Pa., who was a faithful brother to me, and he at once communicated our fears to my friend in Mansfield, Ohio, who promptly transmitted to me the following letter, for which he shall have the gratitude of my whole heart as long as I inhale the breath of life.

Rev. J. H. Fesperman.

Dear Sir and Brother:

I notice in a postal card written to Rev. H. C. Harthcox, that you are afraid that your death may occur before the matter of a farm may be arranged, and now write to say that in case such a thing should occur the same thing will be done for your widow as was proposed for you. That is to say, the same proposition as made will be carried out and will not be interfered with by your death. The money is ready any day. Yours truly,

M. D. Harter.

Soon after this letter reached me Brother Harter employed an attorney, Hon. William Robbins, to see that a perfect title for the land was secured, and then transmitted the following contributions, viz: M. D. Harter, Mansfield, Ohio, $100; G. D. Harter, Canton, Ohio, $100; C. Aultman, Canton, Ohio, $100; A. J. Drexel, Philadelphia, Pa., $100; Geo. W. Childs, Philadelphia, Pa., $100; H. Lloyd, Son & Co., Pittsburgh, Pa., $100; Huntington Brown, Mansfield, O., $10.00; Kountze Bros., New York, $50.00. The First English Lutheran church in Cincinnati, Ohio, gave me seventy-five dollars, St. John's Lutheran church, Charleston, S. C., contributed seventy-five dollars, and others whose names space will not allow me to mention gave smaller sums, until we had eight hundred and fifty dollars, the amount required to pay for the land.

An attorney had the business in hand and the day was appointed to fill out the deed, but alas for poor human nature, the owner, having in some way found out that the money had been given to me by generous friends, at once added fifty dollars to the price he first proposed to take and sent word to me that when this was paid he would make the title. Some one had offered more for the land and this was what made him act in bad faith. This man was a stranger to me, but I considered him a fine representative of "By-ends and Money-love," characters in "Pilgrim's Progress," who when they came to the silver mines of Demas, sacrificed their principles for the sake of worldly profit. Some of my friends went to Mr. K., reasoned with and tried to persuade him to let his original contract with me remain unbroken, but nothing except the extra fifty dollars could move him to make and sign the deed. The money was raised, the title secured, and then double trouble commenced. I had been deceived concerning the cleared land said to have been on the place, and besides the community consisted of illiterate and superstitious people without educational advantages. My children were all young, I was too sick to remain out of bed longer than a few hours each day, the plantation consisted of a body of heavily timbered woodland and I had no money left to build with or improve it in any way. Trusting God, we rented a small house contiguous to the place, moved into it, and every child that could handle an ax or pick brush, immediately commenced clearing land. Our precious Saviour only knows what terrible hardships and great trials we daily endured, but we knew that God reigned and some pious people still lived, and although hope flickered, it did not expire. Almighty God, who watches the flight of angels to the most distant world in His vast dominions and follows the true Christian upon his footstool to the closet, the palace of kings, the wilderness, the dungeon, or the scaffold, or to the cross, raised up the following named churches and friends to contribute in our behalf: Wentworth Street Lutheran Church, Charleston, S. C., through Rev. L. K. Probst, pastor, Mrs. C. Burkhalter, Boschen Bros., William Dodge, Rev. W. H. Keller, some congregations in New York city, Rev. W. H. Settlemyer, Rev. L. A. Mann and a few other friends and brethren. With the economical use of the donations given by these friends, and through hard labor, we managed to erect a house, dig a well, and put up some necessary outbuildings. My family continued to struggle and toil with a determination to open and improve the place. Huge trees were to be cut down, logs rolled and burned, and nobody but children under fourteen years old to do this work,—all this made the accomplishment of our design an overwhelming task, well calculated to fill our hands with daily labor and our minds with deep solicitude. Just as we began to think that success would finally crown the faithful efforts of our family to make a support, long sickness and death entered the "church of our household," took our first-born son, sixteen years old, who was our chief help, and gave him to immortality—transferred him to scenes of unsuffering life and undying glory at God's right hand,

> Where sighs are all out of hearing,
> And tears are all out of sight,
> And the shadows of earth are forgotten
> In the heaven of painless delight.

Our son Bickle was a child of unusual promise, and we cherished bright hopes of this, our first born. His youth was all that life and piety could make it. But the bud of promise had scarcely opened its first petal, when the frost of an early death blighted it forever—no, not forever, for the flower too rich for earth was gathered by the Lord from the waste of life to the heavenly garden. The breaking of the tender stem was, indeed, painful to his body and the smitten hearts of his parents, but Jesus and the resurrection can heal all the bruises and comfort the sorrowing hearts left behind. Without cessation, he suffered intense pain three months and three weeks, during which time he was not once heard to murmur, complain, or wonder why the Lord thus dreadfully afflicted him.

During his sickness he prayed many times that a merciful God would give me my health that I might again preach the gospel of Christ. Knowing that my heart was breaking and fearing that I might be overwhelmed by his death, he called for the Bible and requested me to sit by his side while he read the first chapter in the book of Job. With a feeble voice he read of Job's afflictions and misfortunes, and then looking at me, remarked: "Father, remember that, in all this Job sinned not, neither did he charge God foolishly, and that the Lord gave him his children again." A few days before his death he told us that we would have hard struggles and many severe trials in our new home, but that he would not be here to know it. He expected to become a ministering angel, and when we died he would meet us on the shores of the mystic Jordan. When dying he exclaimed, "Raise me higher," and while his wasted arms encircled our necks for the last time, God sent a messenger from above and took him home,

> Where no parted friends
> Over dying loved ones have to weep;
> Where no bed of death parental love attends,
> To watch the coming of a pulseless sleep.

We laid the body of our beautiful boy in the grave, but we left him not to slumber alone, for we left our hearts with him. Eight years of severe and dangerous bodily affliction have come and gone since that memorable day, when we laid the skeleton form of our child in the dust, and I now hop about on crutches, while each heart throb of my life brings me intense pain, and in this condition I frequently sit down on the decayed stumps of the large trees cut down by the hands of the child who now lies in the grave—cut down at the sacrifice of his life to open the way to provide for me, and I weep as if my heart would break. I cannot refrain from weeping for my faithful son. These pages, dear reader, are abundantly watered by my tears, but the promise he made, "When you and mother die I will meet you on the shores of the mystic Jordan," swallows mortality and bids defiance to the grave. It bids me look up to Him who hears my sighs, counts my tears and feels the great anguish of my suffering heart. When I die I will doubtless see that the afflictions and many ills of my life were but the disguised regards of Almighty goodness, the great shadows of heaven resting upon the vision of earth. When our loved ones die and angels ask for tears at the sight of the heart's fondest ties and most touching affinities rudely wrecked and sundered by the hand of death—at such a moment what single thought of earth or heaven could so increase the sunset splendor of the soul, the cloudless rainbow of the mind, as the felt assurance of reunion in heaven with those we loved and trusted here? We shall still live and love in heaven.

How beautiful is that description by the poet of the parent and children meeting together in heaven :

"And when I saw my little children unchanged,
And heard them fondly call me by my name,
Then is the bond of parent and of child
Unbroken, I exclaimed, and drew them closer to my heart and rejoiced."

After the death and burial of our son my family again resumed labor, enduring many great privations, until hope began to sing her cheerful song, encouraging us to believe that we would at last become self-sustaining. But alas! just then another son, fourteen years old, got hurt while hauling logs, and was made a helpless cripple for life. Physicians expressed the opinion that his injury had produced white swelling, and they cut to the bone below and above the knee joint, making ugly wounds and discovering nothing but blood. This operation produced eryesipelas, and in my opinion killed the bones below and above the joint, and thus brought on true necrosis. This dear son has been a suffering cripple five years. He lay in bed nine months suffering excruciating pain. Honeycombed bones have come out of his limb, and now it is only a question of time when he will have to undergo an amputation. It seems strange that in each case these painful, dangerous and long continued family afflictions completely baffled the skill of many physicians, and bade defiance to all healing art. The doctors seemed unable to fathom the nature of the disease and were powerless even to alleviate the intense sufferings of their patients.

In these family afflictions our work was interfered with and our expenses greatly increased, but the Lord, who is invincible in power and supreme in authority, who gave fragrance and beauty to the flowers and bread to the ravens, that they might be vehicles of mercy to His people, caused Christian friends North and South to remember us in our great and trying troubles. Without solicitation, the First English Lutheran Church in Cincinnati, Ohio, remembered us on four Christmas occasions, each time sending money, clothing, and other useful articles, which lessened the burdens resting upon our weary shoulders and sorrowing hearts.

Louis Manss, of Cincinnati, Ohio, and his faithful Christian family, did much to cheer our troubled minds. Rev. Edmund Belfour, D. D., Rev. J. K. Melhorn and their congregations, Dr. W. A. P——, Pittsburgh, Pa., Trinity Lutheran Church, Lancaster, Pa., Rev. Charles Fry, pastor; Rev. Jacob Fry, D. D., Reading, Pa.; Rev. L. E. Albert, D. D., and his people, Philadelphia, Pa.; St. Mark's Church, Rev. Samuel Laird, pastor, Philadelphia, Pa.; Miss Annie Gundaker, and other Christian friends, came to our rescue and encouraged us by words and deeds of brotherly kindness.

"The least flower with a brimming cup may stand,
And share its dewdrop with another near."

For many years I have been face to face with trouble,—with continuous unbroken mysteries—with bitter disappointment, with personal and family afflictions and bereavement. My cup of sorrow has been filled again and again after I have drained it of its very dregs. Misfortunes of various kinds have followed me, and I have been made to pass through the circle of suffering, but I have submitted all distressing problems to God without questioning, and in the firm faith that He seeks my highest good. I repose on my own heavenly Father's love without demanding to know the reasons for His special dealings with me.

"I do not ask my cross to understand,
My way to see;
Better in darkness just to feel Thy hand,
And follow Thee:
Joy is like restless day, but peace divine
Like quiet night;
Lead me, O Lord, till perfect day shall shine
Through peace to light."

Suffering seems to be the law of my life. There has not been one day in twelve years when I could truthfully say, "I am well." It is given to me to suffer for God's sake. In other worlds I shall more perfectly serve Him and love Him, praise Him, work for Him,

"Grow nearer and nearer Him with all delight;
But then I shall not any more be called
To suffer, which is my appointment here."

I sit with Job in ashes, but I am not comfortless, nor do I regret the day of my birth. To quarrel and fret over my afflictions would not free me from them. That would make them heavier and life more miserable. I cannot ignore them and refuse to recognize them, for they will not down at my bidding. The best physicians have been unable to remove them. They assert themselves in every inch of my body, and thrust themselves across the pathway of my family, destroying the life and health of my children. What can I do with these terrible double afflictions and pressing cares? Peter solves the difficulty by telling me to cast all my care upon God; and herein he only repeats the older advice of the Psalmist, "Cast thy burden upon the Lord." The Bible says, "Who is among you that feareth the Lord, that obeyeth the voice of his servants, that walketh in darkness and hath no light? Let him trust in the name of the Lord, and stay upon his God." "Wait on the Lord; be of good courage, and he shall strengthen thy heart." "Be careful for nothing, but in everything with prayer and supplication, with thanksgiving, let your requests be made known to God." "Cast thy burden upon the Lord, and He shall sustain thee." His promises ask me to lay my burdens upon Him, because He careth for me, and will help me, and strengthen me, and comfort me. With a resigned heart and submissive will I look to God for grace and strength, and rest upon His promises and providences with a submissive spirit. I cannot explain why the Lord permits me to be so sorely afflicted, but I know that my heavenly Father is just, and loving, and true. I transfer my burden of cares upon Him, and they become bonds of union and sources of strength. They teach me to lean on Him more constantly and more lovingly, and so promote and sweeten my communion with Him. He is willing for all His children to lean on Him.

"Sufferer of my love, lean hard,
And let me feel the pressure of thy care;
I know thy burden, sufferer; I shaped it,
Poised it in my own hand, made no proportion
In its weight to thine unaided strength;
For even as I laid it on, I said,
I shall be near, and while he leans on me
The burden shall be mine, not his:
So shall I keep my sufferer within the circling arms
Of mine own love. Here lay it down, nor fear
To impose it on a shoulder which upholds
The government of worlds. Yet closer come;
Thou art not near enough; I would embrace thy care,
So I might feel my sufferer reposing on my breast.
Thou lovest me? I know it. Doubt not, then;
But, loving me, lean hard."

Leaning on Jesus Christ, I rest secure in my place, and exclaim:

"Precious Saviour, more than life to me,
I am leaning hard on Thee;
Through this changing world below,
Sustain me gently as I go."

In the year 1887, soon after my crippled son recovered sufficient strength to use crutches, I was stricken down with valvular heart disease, which for a long time compelled me to occupy a sitting posture in my bed. Many nights my wife sat in the bed and held me, while I reclined on her breast, only sleeping a few moments at a time. This stoppage in the action of my heart arrested the flow of blood to my brain, producing indescribable feelings and great agony of mind. I lay in bed almost the whole of one summer, and the least physical exertion or mental excitement invariably brought on paroxysms of my heart. Physicians who visited me abandoned all hope of my life and told the people in the neighborhood that I could not survive. In their opinion my case was hopeless. While I was in this precarious and helpless condition my youngest son, ten years old, who had gone on an errand to a neighbor's house was carried home screaming and bleeding, and was laid on the bed. The calf of his leg was badly torn by a large and vicious dog. Physicians pronounced the wounds dangerous and with great difficulty stitched the injured parts together. The wounds were carefully dressed every day, and the child suffered a great deal. This misfortune happened in April, 1888, and it was many weeks before he could walk. My home seems a place consecrated by suffering, tears and prayers.

Sorrow is the very woof which is woven into the warp of my life. God created my nerves to agonize and my heart to bleed, and almost every nerve has thrilled with pain, and every affection has been wounded. I have been baptized with affliction, and in it discerned the divine sacredness of sorrow, and the profound meaning which is concealed in pain. How strangely has suffering been meted out to me and to my loved ones. I do not cry out in misery and anguish as Job did, and expostulate with the Most High because of the mysterious visitations. I am willing to be used as His will directs. He does not take away my pain, or heal my sickness; but he gives me strength to bear it, He illumines my suffering life with these promises, "When thou passest through the waters, I will be with thee, and through the rivers, they shall not overflow thee; when thou walkest through the fire, thou shalt not be burned, neither shall the flames kindle upon thee," "Whom the Lord loveth He chasteneth, and scourgeth every son whom he receiveth."

> Claiming these promises,
> Misfortune never can move me,
> No judgment can dismay.
> For Jesus, who doth love me,
> Walks with me day by day.

CHAPTER IV.

On the 14th of January, 1889, I was doomed to suffer the most heart-rending calamity of my unfortunate life. Scarcely able to be out of my bed, I attempted a journey a mile from home, my horse ran away, I was caught in the wheel of the vehicle and my foot, with the exception of the tendon, was torn off, leaving several inches of the bare bone projecting. Immediately after the accident, I sat up and cut off my boot, only to discover that one of my poor feet on which I had traveled hundreds of miles to preach God's Word, was almost entirely separated from my poor frail body. I was taken home to my weeping family in a wagon that had no springs, and every inch of the rough road produced great suffering. Physicians stretched the contracted tendon and let the joint fly back into its socket. This caused me the greatest pain I ever endured. After a few days they put the limb into a box of wheat bran. Fermentation took place and this produced a bad case of mortification. I lay nine days suffering more than human tongue can describe, and the foot turned dark and fell out of socket, leaving the ends of the bones exposed. Two and sometimes three doctors came every day, stood at the foot of the bed and stared at my poor decayed limb. My wife dressed my wounds with greater tenderness and skill than any of the physicians. One day I pointed to the foot as it lay on one side, and to the dark bones as they projected in another direction, and said to the medical men, "Gentlemen, that leg will have to be amputated." They promptly assented. The next day was appointed for the operation. I used every effort to avoid the knives of inexperienced men by telegraphing to skilled physicians in Salisbury, N. C., requesting them to come to my assistance, but the distance, cold, ice and other things prevented them from responding. The attending physicians came at the appointed time, the 23rd of January, 1889, ate their dinners, held a private consultation, and then announced that they were ready to perform the operation. I could not secure the services of more competent men and I was obliged to submit. The house and yard were full of men and even of women, who seemed anxious to witness the amputation. My wife and children kneeled around my bed, while I prayed that a merciful God would take them under His special care, and give me the needed strength to endure the fearful trial just before me. I took each of my weeping loved ones by the hand, blessed them, kissed them and bade them adieu, and then calling for the chloroform, which was administered in large quantities, in a short time I was perfectly oblivious to the world around me. I was one hour under the knives, saw and needles of the doctors. The bones had been severed and I suppose it must have been when the physicians injured a nerve that my consciousness returned, and I immediately knew everything that was being done. The remaining arteries were caught, and the flaps stitched without the use of any more chloroform, and nothing but Almighty power could give me the the ability to describe the awful suffering I endured while this was being accomplished. The operation was finally finished, and I was carried to my bed, but believing that my leg had been cut off where the flesh was unsound, I remarked to the physicians: "You have amputated my limb too low down, in inflamed material and thus ruined me." They replied, "No, Mr. Fesperman, we cut it off there because we knew that when you got well you would desire to wear a pretty little artificial foot."

The doctors in performing the operation had injured a nerve, and made a flap too short, which, being inflamed, quickly sloughed away, leaving the bones and the marrow in them exposed many weeks before any sign of healing appeared. The lack of skill in the administration of the chloroform caused it to take all the skin from my lips, mouth, tongue and throat. My wife took fine linen cloth and wiped the burnt flesh out of my throat and mouth. I expectorated blood and my lungs felt as if they would burn up. The injured nerve in the stump of my leg had the constant sensation of being in a blaze of fire. I am unable to describe the fearful sufferings I endured. Soon after the operation was finished, I commenced sinking and lingered between death and life until the sixth day, when the first sign of improvement appeared.

During this time intervals of consciousness returned, and on each occasion I would feebly inquire: " Where is my baby boy? " The mother, who sat by my side, would answer: " Here he is, with his head on my lap." Looking at him satisfied me, and my mind would then immediately launch out into unconsciousness, and I imagined that angels were flitting round me and that I was walking on the stub of my amputated leg, crossing creeks, rivers and oceans, always carrying my precious child in my arms. I verily believe that the constant presence of this dear boy greatly assisted me to fight a strong battle for life. I had five other children, whom I loved equally well, but he being the youngest, was more constantly on my mind.

My faithful wife sat by my bed and watched me day and night nearly six weeks without any rest except what she obtained by placing her head on my pillow and thus sleeping a few moments at a time. The Lord strengthened her in her vigils by my side.

"God gives His angels charge of those who sleep,
But He Himself watches with those who wake."

The Lord watched by my bedside with my wife and sustained her strength and courage.

"God made suffering the Law of my life,
But He Himself came to me, and stood
Beside me, gazing down on me with eyes
That smiled, and suffered; that smote my heart,
With their own pity, to a passionate peace;
And reached to me Himself the Holy cup,
Saying, 'Intense sufferer, drink with me,'
My pale brow will compel thee, my pure hands
Will minister unto thee; thou shalt take
Of this communion through the solemn depths
Of the dark waters of thine earthly agony,
With a heart that praises Me, that yearns to Me,
The closer through this hour. Hold fast my hand,
Though the nails pierce thine too; take only care
Lest one drop of the sacramental wine
Be spilled, of that which ever shall unite
Thee, soul and body, to thy living Lord.
I will not leave thee, I will not depart,
Nor lose thee, nor forget thee, but will clasp
Thee closer in the thrilling of my arms.
And this terrible pain and agony shall make thee
Serve Me and love Me, praise Me, and work for Me.
And through affliction grow nearer and nearer to Me."

Too weak to raise my head from the pillow, I lay, day and night, communing with my precious Saviour, and every moment suffered excruciating pains. The attending physicians and visiting friends considered my case hopeless. The news that I was standing on the very threshold of the grave—the gateway to my Father's house of many mansions, rapidly spread through the country. Presbyterian and Methodist ministers and their congregations offered special prayers to God for my recovery. This was the second time in my life when the people of different denominations unitedly asked the Lord to heal my sickness. Revs. Bagby and Ivey, Methodist ministers, with whom I had once associated, came in person, knelt by my bed and prayed that Almighty God would graciously strengthen and raise me up again. My faithful friend and esteemed brother, Rev. W. Kimball, hearing of my helpless condition, came from his home near China Grove to visit and comfort me. Bro. Kimball had once been my pastor and his presence did much to encourage me. He promptly sent the following account of my misfortune to the church papers:

"Rev. J. H. Fesperman, a Lutheran minister of the North Carolina Synod, who has been an invalid for nine years, unable to preach or do any labor, sustained a most fearful injury on Monday last. Being weak and sick with heart disease, he started to a neighbor's house in a one-horse wagon. The horse became frightened and ran away. Bro. Fesperman became entangled and his left leg was broken and the foot torn entirely out of the socket, leaving the bone projecting at least three inches, entirely bare of skin. The physicians who set and treated the leg, said in all their practice they had not seen so bad a case. They gave not the least encouragement for his leg or life. The prevailing opinion is that it will have to be amputated, which operation his physical strength will not, we fear, be able to bear. For more than eight years this brother and his family have had almost constant and double affliction, first in his own personal trouble, consumption ; second, the loss of his eldest son ; third, the affliction of the sixteen-year-old son, who has been so badly maimed with white swelling that he is unable to perform any labor. In every instance the affliction has been long and dreadful ; and finally the excruciating calamity which has fallen upon the head of the family, whose feet were near the brink of the grave. Sister Fesperman, in this her great trial, asks the prayers and sympathy of the entire Church of God. Surely those who are being blessed with the abundance of this world's goods will remember this sorely-afflicted brother and family in this time of need.

"W. KIMBALL."

This article from the pen of brother Kimball appeared in several church papers, and Mr. C. T. Bernhardt, of Salisbury, N. C., was the first person to transmit pecuniary aid, which he accompanied with his sincere sympathy. Many of my brethren whose names I would be glad to mention, sent me words of cheer with substantial tokens of their

Christian sympathy. Friends at China Grove, through Rev. W. Kimball, the congregations of Revs. Chas. B. King, Father Rothrock, Wright Campbell, F. W. E. Peschau and William Lutz contributed to sustain me in my desperate affliction and trying trouble. Letters of Christian love and brotherly affection came to me from California, Kansas, Nebraska, and from the east and west, north and south, conveying small sums of money for my benefit, and telling me of prayers that were going up to God in my behalf. These pecuniary gifts provided comforts for myself and family and paid the physicians who visited me every day. Doctors traveled twelve miles each trip they made, and coming every day, even at half rates, amounted to no little expense for me. Revs. Peschau, Kimball and King kept themselves informed of my physical, temporal and spiritual condition, for which they shall ever have my profound gratitude.

> "If none were sick and none were sad,
>   What service could we render?
> I think if we were always glad,
>   We scarcely could be tender.
> Did our friends never need
>   Patient ministration,
> Earth would grow cold and lose, indeed,
>   Its sweetest consolation."

I lay in bed many months not knowing the cause of my ever-present and awful sufferings, until surgeons North, through correspondence, informed me that my main nerve was injured, that each pulsation of my heart rushed the blood to the end of the artery and jerking an attached nerve, produced pain at every throb. If the physicians who performed the operation of amputation, and who visited me every day, knew the cause of my indescribable misery, they preferred to let the secret go with me into the grave, rather than to divulge. Very distinguished surgeons have informed me that the operation of "dividing the nerve" could have been successfully performed if the attempt had been made before the surrounding tissues were diseased. I asked the attending physicians to please explain why I had to suffer perpetual torture, but they replied, "We don't know." The history of succesful amputations develops the fact that after the second or third week the pain gradually disappears. But in my case it has been otherwise. Long and constant suffering has caused a cancerous growth, called a "neuroma," to form under the skin on the end of the injured nerve. This terrible tumor grows, jerks, quivers, pains and burns without cessation, as if the stump of the limb were in a vessel of scalding water, and nothing will bring alleviation. Receiving no relief from physicians in Iredell Co., I commenced corresponding with noted surgeons in Baltimore, Md., and in Richmond, Va., and their answers to my inquiries developed a perfect unanimity of opinion concerning my case. On Friday, July the 2nd, 1889, Rev. F. W. E. Peschau, D. D., of Wilmington, N. C., President of the Evangelical Lutheran Synod of North Carolina, visited me, offered prayer to God in my behalf, and spent several hours of edifying social conversation with me. On Saturday, July the 3rd, Bro. Peschau returned and administered the Holy Communion to myself and family.

> Christ is a living presence everywhere,
> And He has countless means, and voices low and sweet,
> We cannot be where we will not meet
> Some message of His tender love and care.

My dear Saviour comes to me in the Holy Communion and makes common things sacred, and perishable things precious, and dark things bright, and sorrowful things a source of strength, and gladness and safety. If a man's misfortunes excluded him from an acceptable participation in the Lord's Supper, then I should be miserable, but, believing that there is no path so hard, so rough, so lowly, or so dark that he who walks therein may not hope to meet Christ in the way, I remain cheerful, and say,

> " Out of myself, dear Lord,
> O, lift me up!
> No more I trust myself in life's dim maze,
> Sufficient to myself in all its devious ways,
> I trust no more, but humbly at Thy throne
> Pray, ''Lead me, for I cannot go alone."

Out of my weary self,
O, lift me up!
I faint: the road winds upward all the way;
Each night but ends another weary day.
Give me Thy strength, and I may be so blest
As " on the heights " I find the longed-for rest.

Out of my selfish self,
O, lift me up!
To live for others, and in living so,
To be a blessing wheresoe'er I go,
To give the sunshine, and the clouds conceal,
Or let them but the silver clouds reveal.

Out of my lonely self,
O, lift me up!
Tho' other hearts with love are running o'er,
Tho' dear ones fill my lonely home no more,
Tho' every day I miss the fond caress,
Help me to join in others' happiness.

Out of my doubting self,
O, lift me up!
Help me to feel that Thou art always near,
That tho' 'tis night and all around seems drear,
Help me to know that tho' I cannot see,
It is my Father's hand that leadeth me."

CHAPTER V.

As soon as I was able to leave home I had myself conveyed to Salisbury, N. C. Rev. Chas. B. King, pastor of St. John's Lutheran Church, met me at the station, accompanied me to comfortable quarters which he had previously provided, showed me many tender acts of brotherly kindness, and before I left thoughtfully handed me the money to pay my expenses. The physicians examined my limb, expressing the opinion that it would gradually become worse, and that my only hope of relief would be through re-amputation. Although suffering without a moment of cessation, I could not abandon the belief that the nerve and artery could be divided by surgical skill. I knew that the physicians in Salisbury were men of ability, and I returned home much discouraged, only to realize that the belief of the medical men in regard to my case was correct. My sufferings increased, I applied poultices, laudanum, chloroform, ether, cocaine, creosote, oil of peppermint, and everything that suggested itself to my mind, but nothing alleviated the pain a single moment. I wrote to distinguished surgeons and physicians in Baltimore, Md., and in Richmond, Va., giving them a minute description of my case. Some of them expressed the opinion that if they could see me personally they could determine whether it was possible to divide the nerve and artery, and thus relieve me.

I could not hop on my crutches unless my wife or one of my children carried my leg in front of me. This was done by putting a scarf around my limb, holding it up and walking before me. Notwithstanding this, I again went to Salisbury to consult physicians, but they assured me that my condition had grown more critical, and reiterated the opinion that nothing except re-amputation would relieve me. I requested one of the oldest surgeons in Salisbury, who knew the condition of my lungs and heart, to please place himself as if in the very presence of Almighty God, and in such an attitude to express his opinion in regard to my recovery from re-amputation. He quietly and kindly answered: "Mr. Fesperman, prepare everything before you undergo the next operation, for you will expire under the knife." I went away from the surgeon's office with these words on my tongue:

> "All the sorrows, all the ill,
> Which my Heavenly Father's will
> Has already made me bear,
> Or in future may prepare,
> While I run my earthly race,
> I will meet all in its place,
> Bold and cheerful by His grace."

"Get everything ready before you have your leg re-amputated, for you will expire under the knife," were words uttered by an experienced physician, and they had no small influence on my mind. No man possessing a sound mind will rush on death, neither will he risk his life so long as he can avoid it. Being hedged in on all sides by lung and heart troubles, and other difficulties, all of which precluded the thought of safety in undergoing another operation, I resolved to go home, trusting that the day would yet come when I could say, "The Lord hath done all things well. He chose this path for me."

"No feeble chance, nor hard, relentless fate,
  But love. His love, hath placed my footsteps here ;
He knew the way was rough and desolate ;
  Knew how my heart would often sink with fear,
Yet tenderly He whispers, 'Sufferer, I see
    This path is best for thee.'
    He chose this path for me,
And well He knew that I must tread alone
  I's gloomy vales and ford each flowing stream ;'
Knew how my bleeding heart would sobbing moan,
  Dear Lord. to wake and find it all a dream,
Love scanned it all, yet still could say, I see
    This rath is best for thee.
    He chose this path for me.
Even while He knew the fearful midnight gloom,
  My timid, shrinking soul must travel through ;
How towering rocks would oft before me loom,
  And apparitions meet my frightened view
Still comes the whisper, 'Sufferer, I see
    This path is best for thee.'
    He chose this path for me.
What need I more, than this sweet truth to know,
  That all along these strange, bewildering ways
O'er rocky steeps and where dark rivers flow
  His loving arms will bear me 'all the days,'
A few steps more, and I myself shall see
    This path is best for me."

In the summer of 1889, after I returned from my visit to the doctors in Salisbury, my sufferings were so intense that I was liable to the lock-jaw. Being afraid of falling into the hands of incompetent physicians, I determined to move to Salisbury, where I could be near prompt and efficient surgical and medical assistance.

Informing my friend and brother, Rev. Chas. B. King, in whose judgment I had perfect confidence, of my desire to locate in Salisbury, that I might be convenient to physicians there, he selected a comfortable house, situated in a quiet, healthful and good neighborhood, which I rented and moved into in September, 1889. Distinguished surgeons, North, encouraged me to believe that it was possible to relieve me without cutting off the leg another time. But I did not possess a "minister's permit" to travel over the different railroads at reduced rates, and I knew that without this permit the expense of going North to see surgeons would require more money than I was able to command. Here again my esteemed brother, Rev. Charles B. King, did not fail in his friendship or influence. In the face of obstacles that prevented others from asking such a favor for me, he applied for a "Clerical permit" for me to visit Baltimore, and the railroad officials promptly granted his request. Leaving my children in the care of brother King, and accompanied by my wife, I went to Baltimore in October, 1889, entered the Union Protestant Hospital, where we consulted some of the most distinguished surgeons of the city. Soon after our arrival, Dr. Fawcett, the superintendent of the hospital, examined my chest, after which he expressed the opinion that I was indeed in a dangerous condition, and at the same time remarked, that he would not attach any blame to me if I returned home the next day. Dr. Fawcett is an exceedingly agreeable and intelligent man. He treats his patients with fatherly kindness and inspires their confidence. Rev. S. Stall and Rev. W. P. Evans, Lutheran pastors in the city, promptly called on me and proffered their services to aid me in securing the advice of the most talented surgeons in Baltimore. God bless these noble pastors! They assured me of their sympathy and willingness to abide by me. They tenderly informed me that if any operation were performed and I needed pecuniary aid to carry me through long confinement, I might expect them to be true to me. These brethren had the fine sensibility to understand my feelings, and the judgment to know what would be necessary, and they have my profound gratitude for the consideration and attention they showed to me while I lay suffering in their city.

> "Blest is the man
>   Whose breast expands with generous warmth
> A brother's woes to feel,
> And bleeds in pity o'er the wounds
> He needs the power to heal.
>   He spreads his kind, supporting arms
> To every child of grief;
>   His secret bounty largely flows,
> And brings unmasked relief."

Through the help of Brother Stall, I had quick access to the presence of some of the most prominent surgeons in Baltimore. Dr. Allen P. Smith is a distinguished surgeon, and a very kind gentleman. He visited me three times, and I also consulted him in his office, but he considered it impracticable to attempt to relieve me in any way except through re-amputation. The celebrated surgeon, Tiffany, of the University Hospital, richly deserves the great distinction the public confers upon him. He received me with great urbanity, examined my condition with much patience and tenderness, and then with kindness and candor gave me his opinion, saying, "Re-amputation is the only sure remedy for your sufferings. Your pain will gradually increase and become so intense that you will be obliged to remove the limb or expire with it on you. You are here now and can travel about on your crutches, but if I put you on the operating table and re-amputate your leg, you may expire in two minutes. Now, I have given you my opinion, and if you desire me to perform the operation, I will cheerfully go to any place in the city and re-amputate your limb, and if you survive, I will wait on you like a son." I certainly love and reverence this great and noble surgeon for his ability, candor and kindness. When I left the room he accompanied me to the door, offered to assist me on the street car and left the image of his greatness written for all time on my mind. After this interview we deemed it best to return to our children in Salisbury, N. C. Rev. S. Stall, learning of our intention to leave the city, handed us fifty dollars from the "Ministerial Relief Society of Baltimore," which sum amounted to within twenty dollars of the expenses incurred by the trip. We left Baltimore with sad hearts. I had been informed by surgeons of very great ability that my leg was a "sample of miserable surgical inefficiency," that the condition of my lungs and heart made it exceedingly dangerous for me to take chloroform, that the shrunken and diseased state of my muscles and nerves would doubtless cause sloughing to occur, that nothing except re-amputation would free me from constant misery, and that this kind of operation would in all probability quickly prove fatal.

We returned from Baltimore to Salisbury, and found our children well, for which blessing we devoutly thanked our dear Lord. With hope in God and my hold on heaven, I determined to try to bear my sufferings, and to wait and pray, trusting that some remedy might yet be found to alleviate my misery, but my pain gradually became more intense. Day after day, and night after night, I held my withered, painful limb in my hand, and prayed that my precious Saviour, who holds the world on His arm, and the stars in His right hand, would mercifully and speedily deliver me. Thus suffering, without abatement, I concluded to visit a famous surgeon in Richmond, Va., with whom I had corresponded, and who had expressed a willingness to investigate my case. I started out alone and went to Richmond, where the son of Rev. J. S. Moser met me at the station and accompanied me to the parsonage. After resting and taking breakfast, brother Moser went with me to the office of the celebrated surgeon, Hunter McGuire, whom I found surrounded by many suffering patients. Brother Moser announced that I was in the reception room, and the kind surgeon granted me the special favor of an immediate interview. Great surgeons always have their hands full. They have appointed hours for patients to visit them, and those who go into their reception rooms, and find other individuals already there, have to be patient and wait their time Dr. McGuire promptly gave me the opportunity t consult him, and I found him to be a very plain, candid and clever man. After taking me by the hand and requesting me to occupy a seat, he remarked, "I know before I look at your leg what causes your awful suffering, and I fear that nothing can be done to relieve you without greatly endangering your life." He then examined me and expressed the opinion that the doctors who cut off the leg had unintentionally injured the nerve; that the muscles were badly emaciated, and the surrounding tissues diseased; that any attempt to sever the nerve and artery would produce blood poisoning and that nothing but re amputation of the diseased member would afford any relief. He added, "I am not afraid of killing you by the administration of chloroform, but I do fear to apply the knife to that poor leg—that poor leg. I think the flesh will rot off and leave your bones exposed." Discovering the scar where Dr. C. had cut into the stump of my leg, Dr. McGuire remarked, "You have been a very unfortunate man, but in this instance, you were indeed very fortunate that you did not die when the doctor made that useless incision." He then advised me to use a course of electricity, massage and medical treatment, and to be at home with my family when any operation was performed. When I was parting from this eminent surgeon, he kindly requested me to feel myself at liberty to call on him again, and let him know any developments that might take place in my case. After this interview, I returned with Rev. Moser to the parsonage, and spent the remainder of the day in pleasant social conversation. To me, this was a day of great bodily pain, but the dear brother and his good wife did much to cheer my anxious mind, and thereby, to some extent, helped me to bear my physical sufferings without complaint.

Discouraged by the opinion of the surgeon, I concluded to return home as early as possible. Brother Moser kindly secured a berth in a sleeping car for me, and bidding adieu to this family of faithful friends, I left Richmond, and by daylight next morning was not far from my home and family in Salisbury. My return from Richmond without relief was a sore disappointment to me.

> "O blows that smite! O hurts that pierce
> This shrinking heart of mine!
> What are ye but the Master's tools
> Forming a work divine?
> O hopes that crumble to my feet,
> O joy that mocks and flies,
> What are ye but the clogs that bind
> My spirit from the skies?"

Several weeks after I came home from Virginia, Dr. McGuire requested Rev. J. S. Moser to write and say to me, that he would come to Salisbury and re-amputate my leg if he thought he could be of any more service to me than other efficient surgeons, but that he would again advise me to have my family and friends with me when the operation was performed. To me, this counsel was plain enough, and I immediately turned to the twenty seventh page in the Book of Worship and read these soul-inspiring words:

"Give to the winds thy fears,
  Hope, and be undismayed;
God hears thy sighs and counts thy tears;
  He shall lift up thy head.

Through waves, and clouds and storms,
  He gently clears thy way;
Wait thou His time, so shall this night,
  Soon end in joyous day."

To add to my burden of ever present pain and mental anxiety, my afflicted son's disease grew worse, and physicians informed me that his leg would have to be amputated. Notwithstanding paroxysms of great pain he was not willing for the operation to be performed, and I did not feel justifiable in pressing him to submit. I knew what an awful thing it was to endure the pain and shock and extreme weakness invariably produced by a surgeon's knife. It is a dreadful thing to have our flesh cut to pieces and our bones severed, and I will not persuade my son to undergo an operation.

I do not understand the mystery of this double and dreadful affliction. But standing in the light of the nineteenth century, with the Bible for my rule of faith and practice, I believe that every single soul, sick or well, has a place in the heart, and is taken into account in the purposes of Him who moves the tempest, and makes His sun shine upon the unthankful and on the good. These dreadful personal and family afflictions would make me wretched indeed, if I did not believe that the Almighty arranges everything pertaining to me and mine. Skeptics can ask me hundreds of questions about God's providence that I cannot answer, but I shall believe until the day of my death that no pang ever seizes me but God decides when it shall come and when it shall go, and that I am· overarched by unerring care, and that though the heavens may fall, and the earth may burn, and the judgment may thunder, and eternity may roll, if I am God's child, not so much as a hair shall fall from my head, or a shadow drop on my path, or a sorrow transfix my heart, but to the very last particular it shall be under my Father's arrangement. This enables me to anchor and rest my soul fast and firm in God all the day long ; and grasping His hand, to look out on all my mysterious, double and dreadful afflictions and say : " Thy will be done on earth," if not yet " as done in heaven," still done in the issues and events of all, and done with cheerful obedience and thankful acceptance of its commands and allotments in my own suffering life. Thank God, amid my intense agony, the victory of faith triumphs, giving me entire submission to the will of the Lord ; I can truly say :

> "Pain's furnace heat within me quivers,
>   God's breath upon the flame doth blow,
> And all my heart in anguish shivers,
>   And trembles at the fiery glow ;
> And yet I whisper, As God will,
> And, in the hottest fire, hold still.
>
> He comes and lays my heart, all heated,
>   On the hard anvil, minded so,
> Into His own fair shape to beat it,
>   With His great hammer, blow on blow ;
> And yet I whisper, As God will,
> And at His heaviest blows hold still.
>
> He takes my softened heart and beats it;
>   The sparks fly off at every blow ;
> He turns it o'er and o'er and heats it,
>   And lets it cool, and makes it glow ;
> And yet I whisper, As God will,
> And in His almighty hand hold still.
> When God has done His work in me,
> Lo! I say, trusting, As God will,
> And trusting to the end, hold still."

This full acceptance of the divine will in regard to my personal and family afflictions, I consider the law of my life, and the best tribute of homage that I can pay to the Most High God. I find myself where I am, and as I am ; because I am sick and crippled, I need not be useless and unhappy. I accept my situation as of divine appointment, and I try to be content in it. Lamenting over the past will do no good. I cannot recall or change it. Complaining of the present will not mend it. It may make myself and others wretched. Anxiety about the the future will not make it any brighter. My heavenly Father has permitted me to be afflicted, and allowed things to be just as they are. He knows what is best. I know He loves me. I will therefore leave all with Him. No rebellion shall be cherished in my heart, and no murmur shall escape my lips. My Saviour has promised that His grace shall be sufficient for me. He will never leave me, but be a present help in time of suffering. Trusting in Him and committing all to His loving care, I will do what I can to praise Him. I will make the place where my lot is cast as bright and cheerful as I can, and wait with patience, saying, "As God will." While I remained in Salisbury during the spring of 1890, I enjoyed the blessed privilege of sitting under the ministry of Rev. Charles B. King. Brother King delivered beautiful and precious discourses, well calculated to enable me to endure my intense sufferings and to bear my great burden of cares in cheerful, loving trust. This minister of Jesus Christ and ever faithful brother, published the following article covering my visit to Baltimore, and also gave an account of my physical condition:

"There has been no published notice given concerning our afflicted brother Fesperman for about six months. Some of his distant friends have expressed a desire that public mention be made concerning his condition. This request accounts for the following statements: Rev. J. H. Fesperman moved from Barium Springs to Salisbury, N. C., the first of October, 1889, to obtain medical advice and treatment, since he continued to suffer great pain, occasioned by the sad accident in which his left foot and ankle were torn off, and the unsucessful amputation of the limb. On account of his weak physical condition, the physicians in Salisbury could promise him little encouragement in case of re-amputation. He therefore decided to go to Baltimore for further consultation. He spent ten days in Baltimore the latter part of October. While there he consulted the most distinguished surgeons in the city. Their unanimous opinion was, that on account of his heart trouble and lung trouble he would most likely expire under the operation of a second amputation. He was advised to return home and await future developments, and that if the suffering became intense beyond undurance, to submit to another amputation as a last hope. The skilled physicians in Salisbury agree, in the main, with the Baltimore men. Brother Fesperman's present condition is critical. His constant sufferings grow more painful each day, and unless there be some unexpected change very soon, he thinks that he cannot long survive. His stay in Salisbury has been necessarily accompanied by considerable expense. This expense has been borne almost entirely by a few interested friends. Six months' association and sympathy with the brother have brought me into a full knowledge of his condition and trials. These statements are given to inform the brethren, and to lay the facts upon their conscience."

Charles B. King,
Pastor of Lutheran Church, Salisbury, N. C.

This article from Brother King's pen brought from Messrs. Carr, Watts, Strouse, Trout and others, means sufficient to pay my house rent, and bear other expenses while we lived in Rowan Co. Not finding any employment for my children in Salisbury we returned home, where they could work on the farm, and where I spent the summer of 1890 in awful misery. The "neuroma" on the limb kept growing, quivering and jerking, while the injured nerve seemed to be on fire. I spent many nights holding my leg in an elevated position, and when I slept at all, I frequently dreamed of being fast in piles of logs on fire, and in vessels of boiling water from which I could not escape. Day after day, and night after night I writhed in perfect torture and longed for cool weather to come, fully believing that then I would risk every danger and have some operation performed. I could not and would not say that I intended to take my case in my own hand and have the leg re-amputated, even if I should die. I try to be ruled by the indications of Divine Providence. A man came into my house and found me holding my limb and enduring extreme pain. "Mr. Fesperman, why don't you have your leg cut off? I am diseased, but to-morrow I shall go to Baltimore, where the doctors don't kill people, and take my case in my own hand and have a critical operation performed even if it kills me." He did as he declared he would, and now lies in the grave. Not so with me, no, no, God afflicted me for some great purpose. What He does is right. I have been afflicted eleven years—suffering indescribable misery three years, and when the hand of God is reached out to deliver me from pain or restore my health to me, He will open the way and give me the courage to lie down under the knives of surgeons.

 I shrink and shudder at the surgeon's knife—
  Each nerve recoiling from the cruel steel,
 Whose edge seems searching for the quivering life;
  Yet to my sense the bitter pangs reveal
 That still, although the trembling flesh be torn,
  This through God's power can be borne.

Some people have said to me, "If I suffered as you do, I would not hesitate an hour. I would quickly have a physician to remove my limb." Such language is rash—I pray that God may direct what is best for me to do in regard to my condition. I shall prayerfully look to Him, trusting that He may direct me. Not that I mean to be stubborn, I am always glad to receive advice from my dear friends. Indeed I often need counsel in regard to temporal and spiritual things. I crave it, and am heartily grateful for it, but when it comes to a case involving life, this all belongs to God and not to myself or the doctors. We may be instruments, but God is the power.

> "The gifts of birth, death, genius, suffering,
> Are all for God's hand only to bestow,
> I receive my portion and am satisfied."

In the fall of 1890 I was suffering without abatement, and I determined to obtain the best surgical advice. Through correspondence I made arrangements to have a personal interview with some of the most eminent surgeons in Philadelphia, Pa. Writing an application to the Richmond and Danville railroad, I solicited a pass for myself and wife to travel over their roads to Philadelphia, Pa. I went personally to John W. Webb, Esq., the courteous agent in Salisbury, who received me with Christian kindness, read my application carefully, approved and forwarded it to the officials of the railroad, and in a short time we received a pass to and from Philadelphia, Pa. Messrs. Webb, Turk and Taylor, officials of the Richmond and Danville railroad, have the profound gratitude of my heart for the generous kindness they manifested toward me in my affliction.

In November, 1890, we again returned to Salisbury for the purpose of locating our children where in case of sickness they could be near medical aid, and where the pastor of St. John's Lutheran Church could occasionally see that they were well and prospering while we were absent under the care of surgeons. But every time we had necessary arrangements for the journey about completed; providential hindrances prevented us from leaving home. This interference with our plans was noticed by our friends, and some of them pleaded with us to abandon the trip. Once when we were on the eve of leaving home for Philadelphia we received a letter informing us that our daughter at Mount Pleasant was very low with typhoid fever, and that it was necessary to come to her immediately. We hastened thither immediately, to find her indeed dangerously ill, and spent three weeks by her bedside. This severe sickness and other unavoidable things detained us until the limits of our railroad permit expired. We enclosed and returned the pass to the proper authorities, respectfully asking them to extend its limits, and they kindly granted our request. In March, 1891, we committed ourselves, our children, and all our interests into the keeping of Jesus Christ, and went to Philadelphia, Pa. Rev. W. M. Baum, D. D., kindly gave me a letter of introduction to the celebrated Dr. Hayes Agnew, and he was the first surgeon I visited. He received me cordially, and after looking at my limb, remarked, "You must have a very strong mind to endure such a terrible affliction so long and not go insane. It is indeed wonderful that you did not lose your sight and mind, and die in less than six weeks after your leg was amputated and fixed up in that manner. It is God's work that you lived thus long. That knot on the stump of your limb is a neuroma, brought on by an injured nerve, and that leg will continue to get worse. Let me give you my advice, cut it off—the sooner the better. You can take ether if skillfully administered. I will perform the operation for you if you go to the Pennsylvania Hospital." Dr. Agnew stands at the head of his profession in Philadelphia, and like all great men is modest and plain. Dr. Garretson, the next surgeon I met, is a man of fine countenance, and simple and agreeable manners. When he received my letter of introduction he immediately walked into the reception room and gave me a very hearty welcome. He examined the limb and said, "dissect the flap, and thus try to save the leg; and if this will not give relief cut off three or four inches of the bones." When I left he kindly remarked that there would be no pecuniary value attached to any surgical operation he might be able to do for me. Rev. Samuel Laird, D. D., made arrangements for me to see Dr. Henry Beates, a distinguished young surgeon who is a member of St. Mark's Lutheran Church in Philadelphia. Dr. Beates received me with a degree of cordiality that was as grateful to me as it was unexpected. He made me feel at home the moment he had shaken hands with me. I found in him a beautiful instance of intelligence, simplicity, generous feeling, and true dignity. He pronounced my amputated limb to be a "piece of miserable surgical ignorance," and said that if it was his leg he would cut it off above the knee as soon as possible, but that it was necessary for me to take medical treatment previous to an operation. Dr. E. Goodman, chief of the faculty of the Orthopedia Hospital, is a large man with fine head, face and mind. He is a member of the Church of the Holy Communion, a Lutheran congregation, of which Rev. J. A. Seiss, D. D., is the honored pastor.

He examined me at his residence and then requested me to meet the faculty of the Hospital, which I did next day. Dr. Goodman said to his associates: "I examined that leg at my house last night and have thought much about it. I desire, if possible, to keep the knife away from it." Another surgeon quickly responded: "Is the gentleman afflicted with consumption or heart disease?" Dr. Goodman replied: "Well, well, there is evidently something wrong with his chest, and we wish to avoid the knife." A third surgeon immediately inquired: "Doctor, what can you substitute for the knife?" Dr. Goodman answered: "Try electricity, massage, and medical treatment six weeks and if these things do no good, come to us and we will take the dreadful leg off without money and without price. Poor man, how he suffers! Here, nurse, put rubbers on his crutches and bring me woolen bandages, that I may dress his leg, and then show him our rooms that he may know what kind of hospital we keep. I am sorry he did not come to this place immediately after his arrival in Philadelphia."

After I looked through the hospital I, too, was sorry, for I found it to be neat and clean, and in every way well arranged. The nurses were intelligent and accommodating, and the whole institution bore evidence that it was directed by able and good men.

When I bade adieu to Dr. Goodman he said: "Try to bear your terrible sufferings without the use of morphine, for it is the very spirit of the evil one. You deserve credit for not using it to alleviate your intense pain." After this interview I met many other prominent surgeons, all of whom pronounced my condition critical and expressed the opinion that it was necessary for me to take medical treatment previous to an operation.

I also formed the acquaintance of four Lutheran pastors and two Lutheran ladies while I was in Philadelphia. Rev. W. M. Baum, D. D., Rev. Samuel Laird, D. D., Rev. J. L. Sibole, and Rev. Edward E. Sibole visited me in my room and gave me much important information concerning the hospitals and most eminent surgeons in the city.

By invitation I visited Rev. Dr. Baum at his home, and he gave me not only a courteous, but very cordial reception; and the impressions which I had received concerning him were fully justified by his bland and engaging manner, and the elevated tone of his conversation. I should think him rather above the middle size, and in his countenance there was so much of both intelligence and benignity that it was difficult to say which had the preponderance. He was very sociable, and yet his mode of talking was quiet and gentle, and as far removed as possible from anything like pretension. As we talked with him we found that the preacher was gradually giving way to the kind and obliging friend; and we had scarcely spent half an hour in his company before every idea of the stranger was gone and we felt a degree of freedom, mingled with reverence, which might very well have been the growth of years.

Rev. Samuel Laird, D. D., who visited us several times, is a tall, erect man, with a countenance indicative of great vigor of mind and strength of purpose, and with manners the most unstudied and familiar.

Rev. Edward Sibole, who also came to see me, is a fine man, and united in his manner great dignity and seriousness, with simplicity and affability.

Rev. J. L. Sibole, who visited us more frequently than any other pastor in Philadelphia, is a man of great simplicity of manner, entire freedom in conversation, excellent judgment and a heart overflowing with generous impulses. I was greatly impressed with his simple and cordial manners and felt from the moment he entered my room a conviction that he was indeed a brother in Christ who truly sympathized with me in my sore affliction.

His prayers in my behalf, though simple as the language of childhood, were yet so rich in evangelical thought, and withal so beautiful and faultless in expression, that it was difficult for me to believe that they had not been elaborated with devout care. These prayers were exceedingly appropriate, and comforting. I look back to my brief association with this devout Christian brother, with grateful and pleasant recollections.

I had consulted many eminent surgeons and they all decided that my leg would have to be reamputated, and some of them impressed upon me the great necessity of taking medical treatment prior to such an operation. But I was not prepared to remain in the city six weeks to take the treatment mentioned. Hospitals where the patient will permit his body to become material for the knives of inexperienced young surgeons, or students in surgery, will allow low rates of board to those who enter their walls and accept their treatment. I had already acquired sufficient bitter experience to be fully aware of what dreadful suffering surgical knives in the hands of inexperienced men could bring upon mankind, and I was constantly on my guard. There was not a distinguished surgeon in Philadelphia that examined my limb who would have charged me anything for his services, but every one of them preferred to perform the operation in a hospital. Learning that room and board in a well arranged and properly manned hospital would cost myself and wife each from fifteen to twenty dollars per week, and being among strangers, and not having a sufficient amount of money to remain and take the six weeks' treatment previous to an operation, we decided to return home, where we now suffer, pray and await the will of our precious Saviour. We can truly say, God bless the surgeons in Philadelphia, Pa., for they treated us with great delicacy of feeling and kindness of heart. Some of them remarked to me, "The world cannot know your terrible sufferings, but we understand the intensity of your pain and we pity you. We cannot relieve you in any way except to remove your leg, and this kind of operation will greatly endanger your life." Thus situated I do not seek to understand the mystery of my trials—

> "But blindfolded and alone I stand,
>   With unknown thresholds on each hand;
> The darkness deepens as I grope,
>   Afraid to fear, afraid to hope;
> Yet this one thing I learn to know
>   Each day more surely as I go,
> That doors are open, ways are made,
>   Burdens lifted, or are laid,
> By some great law unseen, and still,
>   Unfathomed purposes fulfill,
>   'Not as I will.'
>
> Blindfolded and alone I wait,
>   Loss seems too bitter, gain too late;
> Too heavy burdens in the load,
>   And too few helpers on the road;
> And joy is weak and grief is strong,
>   And years of bitter pain, so long, so long,
> Yet this one thing I learned to know,
>   Each day more surely as I go,
> That I am glad the good and ill
>   By changeless law are ordered still,
>   'Not as I will.'

"Not as I will!" the sound grows sweet
  Each time my lips the words repeat;
'Not as I will,' the darkness feels
  More safe than light when this thought steals
Like whispered voice to calm and bless
  All unrest and all loneliness,
'Not as I will,' because the One
  Who loved me first and best is gone
Before me on the road, and still
  For me must all His love fufill !
    'Not as I will.' "

I had gone to Baltimore, Md., Richmond, Va., Phildelphia, Pa., where I had consulted the most eminent surgeons in the United States without obtaing any relief, and it was quite natural for me to return home under a great weight of disappointment and sorrow, but no grief is so crushing and hopeless that happiness may not again visit the heart where trust and love abide. I was greatly disappointed because I had not realized any benefit —my trips had been fruitless,—but I remembered these men who went stumbling along the road to Emmaus, weeping and mourning that their Christ was gone, poured into His very ear the tale of their bereavement. They told him of their trouble, that they had lost Christ; and there He was talking to them. In the midst of their deep grief was their victory, and they did not know it. Everything seemed to cut off all prospect of relief for me, but trusting the divine promise, "I will never leave thee, nor forsake thee," I made the name of Jesus Christ, the answer to all my doubts, the spring of all my courage, the earnest of all my hopes, the charm omnipotent against all my disappointments, the remedy for all my sickness, the supply for all my wants, and fullness for all my desires,

> "My hope is built on nothing less
> Than Jesus' blood and righteousness,
> I dare not trust the sweetest frame,
> But wholly lean on Jesus' name;
> On Christ the solid rock I stand;
> All other ground is sinking sand."

Being once more in the midst of my family and friends, and suffering increased pain, I fully resolved that after the meeting of the North Carolina Synod, when Pastor King and other brethren could be with me, I would run all risks and have my limb re-amputated. While I was waiting, a boy in the town had his leg successfully amputated and the time consumed in the operation caused me to decide not to have anything done to my limb until I could no longer bear my pain. I knew that if the surgeons North were correct, I could not lie an hour or more under the influence of chloroform and survive its effects. It affords me pleasure to state that while I lived in Salisbury, Rev. Charles B. King and wife, Reissner Brothers, William Smithdeal and Mr. and Mrs. Seyffert showed me Christian kindness. Miss Katie and Mr. George Seyffert, two excellent young people, members of the Lutheran church in Salisbury, did much to encourage me. In June, 1891, I returned to my home in Iredell county, where I spent the summer in perpetual torture. My nights have been fruitful sources of imaginations. For nearly three years my sleep has been nothing but a series of "cat-naps." During my wakeful hours I pray, and listen to the clock as it ticks time away. I think of hospitals, surgeons and their knives, and speculate and wonder how I would feel if I were free from the pain that comes to me with each heart throb of my suffering life. My memory recalls the time when I did not know this awful misery—the time when I went out to visit and comfort the sick, and to preach Christ to perishing sinners, and I look forward to the future without prospect of relief. I remember the pleasures and sorrows I have experienced, the smiling faces I have seen, the incidents that have fallen here and there along my life, like sunlight through a prison; the books that I have read, the places I have visited, the persons I have met, the friendships I have formed, the lands that I have seen, the hearts that I have gladdened, or that have gladdened mine. I recall the old fireside and the faces that used to be there, the times when I have knelt at my mother's loom and prayed for her life, or sat down at the table when the children were children still, when as yet there was no new-made grave in the church-yard. I count the many faces I have seen in sorrow; the eyes in tears, the broken ties I have known, the dear ones in mourning and the number of graves along the pathway of my life. I think of my youthful days, when I lay with a broken leg and gave my heart to the Saviour, and afterwards came forward to the Lord's table for the first time. I remember how I watched and prayed by the bedside of a dying child—how he said "I will meet you on the shores of the mystic Jordan,"—how with slow movement I wended my way to that sacred spot where the rich and the poor meet together—how with utterances of grief that no earthly power could suppress, I witnessed the burial of my first-born son and how I rode home with a broken heart. As in pain, I recall these things, I do not forget that years have rolled away and that I am fast stepping toward the sunset of my life. Life has been to me a vale of suffering and tears, but I have the great Comforter near. I cannot sink to rest like the valiant prophet of old, with my eyes undimmed and my natural force unabated; neither can I be like Caleb, as strong at fifty-two as at forty. I am approaching the gates of silence like Jacob, leaning on my staff. But like David I sing in my confidence, "And now, O Lord, what wait I for, my hope is fixed in Thee."

I am liable at any moment to sudden and violent attacks of other maladies than the diseased nerve whose constant grip holds me in perpetual pain— sinews, joints, muscles, heart, lungs and stomach are more or less involved. My lungs hurt me, and when my heart throbs hard and fast there is thundering in my ears like the beating of a distant drum; but nothing gives me so much agony as the stump of my amputated leg. The very flesh seems to be tearing itself away from the ends of the bones, and I cannot conquer or even alleviate the pain. There is a constant burning cramp around the end of the severed bones which makes my life wretched beyond all description. Occasionally, some strong and hearty, but thoughtless man looks on and will say, when I am writhing in extreme pain, "Don't think about your pain." What would have been the feelings of the sufferers in a recent railroad wreck, if some stout, thoughtless man had stood on the bank of the creek, looking at the piled-up cars, mingling water and blood, and listening to the groans of the dying and cries of the living, and at the same time had said, "This is nothing but a wreck, you have only fallen ninety feet, do not think about your condition! When you feel the flames do not think about your pains." I have only had one or two such comforters, but their advice, kindly meant and injudiciously expressed, did not overthrow my spiritual equilibrium. One of the good effects of affliction is that through its mellowing influences our hearts go out in a more tender sympathy towards others who suffer, and perhaps sweet flowers of pity and compassion will spring up in the wet furrows which never bloomed there before. The well and prosperous scarcely know how to sympathize with the afflicted and unfortunate. It is just those who have passed through some crushing trial and received a baptism of suffering who are the first to sympathize with others who pass under the rod. "One tear of sympathy makes the whole world kin." Until men's own hearts are touched with sorrow, they often fail to give to others that beautiful and tender sympathy which falls upon the stricken heart like the refreshing dews upon earth, when parched and blasted with summer drouth. I once heard a useful pastor say, "I have read the burial service over many dead children and returned from the church yard not thinking any more about what I had been engaged in, but after I followed one of my own children to the grave, I was able to sympathize with other bereaved parents. When I was well and strong I frequently visited sick parishioners without entering into full sympathy with them, but, Brother Fesperman, since the hand of affliction disabled me, two years ago, my sympathies have been aroused for other sufferers." The brother who related this experience to me was a faithful Christian minister, but had always been a hearty man and until stricken down with disease was not able to realize what a thorny road the afflicted have to tread. "It was necessary for some of the trials of life to act upon this dear brother's Christian graces and cause them to send out their fragrance for the refreshment of others,"

> "The good are better made by ill—
> As odors crushed are sweeter still.
> Affliction is the Christian man's shining scene;
> Health and prosperity conceal his brightest ray;
> As night to stars, misery lustre gives to man."

I never knew the time when my heart did not reach in tender pity and compassion after suffering humanity, and now in my varied and severe afflictions, I have the comfort of knowing that I enjoy the sympathy of men and women, and more especially of children. I often share the simple and free, tender and reverent sympathies of children. They watch my face and movements as I hop on my crutches, and I have overheard them say, "I wish I could give him back his foot and make him well and happy again." Out of the mouths of children, the loving and the pure in heart, God has given me strength and comfort. To be great in God's kingdom is to be a little child in the sympathy of faith and the purity of love. Among the happy experi-

S

ences of my suffering life are the friendships I have formed. God who lives and reigns not only here, but also where the compass of design has yet to circumscribe the paths of new created worlds, and the strong pinioned seraph, moving rapid as the light can never, never reach, has cemented and made stronger the friendship of my brethren in North Carolina, and caused friends, whose faces I have never seen, by letters, by messages, by contributions, and by books, to knock at my door and enter in thus bringing joy and comfort to my troubled heart.

> "I have some treasured letters,
>   Fragments of the sympathies of other's lives—
> Precious relics, of friends not yet departed,
>   Friends whose memory still survives.
> Touched by neither time nor distance,
>   Will their words unspoken last;
> Voiceless whispers of the present,
>   Silent echos of the past.
> Such a little thing—a letter,
>   Yet so much it may contain ;
> Written thoughts and mute expressions,
>   Full of pleasure, and sometimes fraught with pain."

I read and re-read these precious letters which conveyed to me the Christian sympathies, kind greetings, best wishes and loving prayers of my brethren and friends, and it gives me renewed energy to pray on and be patient in my sufferings.

During the spring and summer of the year 1891,

Rev. George A. Cox and Rev. Chas. B. King, President and Secretary of the North Carolina Synod, laid me under obligations by assisting me in an official capacity. Mr. William Pore and his now sainted wife deserve my deep gratitude for special kindness manifested toward me and a dear member of my family. The Rinker sisters, Hon. J. A. Gaisenhainer, James Fellows, Esq., Rev. Dr. Belfour, Rev. J. P. Krechting, Rev. Jeremiah Zimmerman, Mrs. Lizzie Funk, friends in Erie, through F. H. Schutte, Esq., Rev. Theo. B. Roth and Rev. G. W. Critchlow have helped and strengthened us. We have received from them words of affection, of guidance, of comfort, which have been, as water in the desert, more precious than gold. There is a hallowed character in this friendship which gives it a warmth and sacredness unknown to the world. It is the cherished enjoyment of Christian friendship that fills my breast with some of its most delightful emotions. Next to the love of Christ, how sweet to love His disciples, to mingle our sympathies with theirs, to interchange evidences of affection, to repose in each other's faithful counsels, and to pray for spiritual blessings on each other's behalf. In the friendship and sympathy of my fellow men I plainly see the footsteps of that great God who is indeed the only Restorer of the hopes and Deliverer of the souls of men, who has promised to hear the prayers of His suffering people, and whose omnipotence marshals suns and systems without name or number, filling with life and gilding with light myriads of worlds untraveled by the wing of seraph, unvisited by the thought of man. I verily believe that Almighty God has manifested special providential care for me through the instrumentality of my Christian friends who have provided for my bodily needs. And I must sincerely pray that as they remembered, cheered and assisted me in my continued, desperate personal and family afflictions, even so may our dear Lord Jesus Christ, who holds the stars in His right hand, listens to the cry of the outcast raven, eyes the sparrow's fall, numbers the hairs on our heads, and gives even to the thirsty worm its dew drop, remember, cheer and fill their hearts with great peace and joy when they lie on their death beds, and then receive them amid the rejoicings of the harvest of the souls of His happy children.

> "Blest are the men whose feelings move
> And meet with generous sympathy and love;
> From Christ the Lord shall they obtain
> Like sympathy and love."

I doubt whether there is another case of domestic affliction and extreme personal suffering similar to mine in the United States. One of the surgeon's in Baltimore, Md., after obtaining my permission for two young physicians to be called into the room to see me, said: "Gentlemen, I know you never looked at a leg resembling this, and I doubt whether you ever see another like it. It is wholly out of the line of all surgical operations, and will never get well. It will get worse and worse, and a very unhappy feature in this truly unfortunate case is that the gentleman is hedged in by other diseases, cutting him off from enduring another operation." A few doctors in the common walks of life are reluctant to express their opinion concerning the operation performed on my limb, 'but the eminent surgeons North and South who have examined me immediately divulge the secret of my terrible and prolonged sufferings. They also tell me that the "heroic effort of trying to secure relief through re-amputation would in all probability at once prove fatal to my life." Such information imparted by men distinguished in their professions is well calculated to make my heart ache, but I still trust God. My present condition is calculated to discourage me, but there is a peace born of struggle, a victory secured by defeat. As day by day I hop on my crutches, carrying my painful limb in a scarf of cloth suspended round my neck, looking out upon the world, in which I shall never take an active part again, I feel this compensation, that a spark of the eternal world dwells in my feeble frame. Whatsoever befalls the hairs that get gray and thin, the withered leg that pains me day and night, the wrinkled hands and the heart that is worn out by much beating, and the blood that clogs and clots at last, and the eyes that are now fast failing, and all the corruptible frame, yet I shall not all die, but deep within this crumbling transient house of clay that must fall and be resolved into the elements out of which it came, there dwells the immortal guest, an ember of eternity, which the ignorance of men can not destroy.

" The leaves of the oak and the willows shall fade,
Be scattered around and together be laid;
And the young and the old, and the low and the high
Shall moulder to dust and together shall lie."
The hand of the king that the sceptre hath borne,
The brow of the priest that the mitre hath worn,
The eye of the sage and the heart of the brave
Are hidden, not lost, in the depths of the grave,
For God has set eternity in the hearts of men.

My soul as well as my body has a history. The spark of eternity within me is by far the most important part of my existence. I have two lives—the outer life of sense and suffering—the inner, hidden life and story of my soul. Beneath the vicissitudes and fluctuations of this crippled body a deep current runs. My visible and frail material life is but the scaffolding under which the eternal life is rearing. The world, that notes the outward events and incidents of my unfortunate life, discerns, after all, but a part, and that the most insignificant part of the history of my being. I might narrate the story of my past life and describe with all minuteness in what spot I was born, in what places and houses I dwelt, what position in society I occupied, what profession I followed, what money I gained or lost, through what external changes of health and sickness, prosperity and adversity, I passed : however interesting or uninteresting it might be to contemplate the strangely diversified allotments of my being, yet after all, in narrating them, they would leave still untouched the half, and by far the more important half of my real life. There has been from the dawn of my existence a mental as well as a material history—a life of the soul, a course of inward progress, a series of changes in the character of that mysterious dweller within my breast more worthy to be chronicled, fraught with interest deeper, more momentous far than the misfortunes and vicissitudes of my outward career. However stirring may be the narrative of my outward experience with heart disease and consumption, broken and amputated legs, crippled children and injured nerves, consultations with surgeons and ever-present pain, there is, to myself, a deeper pathos, a more awful and absorbing interest in the history of the struggles of my soul. My poor physical life has been tossed about, as by some great battle weapon wielded by giant powers in mockery, but in this better part of my existence—this little world in my bosom, there is a seed of eternity which rises up through ignorance, animalism, clay, up through fear, failure, blindness, up through bereavement, double affliction, constant pain, sorrow and sin, up toward light and liberty, bearing in itself the germ of heaven, quickened by the Eternal Spirit and attracted by the ever-living Son of God who causes all hindrances, to become helps and all defeats victories.

> "Oh happy soul that lives on high
> While men lie groveling here,
> His hopes are fixed above the sky
> And faith forbids his fear.
> His conscience knows no secret stings,
> While grace and joy combine
> To form a life, whose holy springs
> Are hidden and divine."

During twelve years my life has been one of constant suffering caused by various maladies, but with all its sorrows and pains, its fightings and fears, its tribulations in the world, its severe chastenings from a Father's hand, it has been the life of a believer in the Lord Jesus Christ.

> I can reach no higher than the Son of God,
> The perfect Head and Pattern of mankind,
> "Perfect through suffering," my salvation's seal
> Set in front of His humanity.

Every pure thought that rises in my breast is

Christ's suggestion; every holy desire and resolution, the proof that He is at hand; every kindling of the spirit into devotion, the unconscious recognition by the spirit of His heavenly presence near. His presence and love cheer me in langour, sustain me in weariness, soothe me in sorrow and nerve me to endure constant pain without murmuring. Whether sleeping or waking, by night and by day, pain is ever-present with me. I enter the house of God suffering pain. I hear the singing, prayers, and preaching under the influence of pain, and in pain remember what I once was—an active minister of Jesus Christ—what I am now—a suffering believer in Christ—and what I shall hope to be in the world to come—a happy soul saved by the precious blood of the Lord Jesus Christ.

> "My pleasures rise from things unseen,
> Beyond this world and time,
> Where neither eyes nor ears have been,
> Nor thoughts of mortals climb."
> "My hopes are fixed on joys to come;
> Those blissful scenes on high
> Shall flourish in immortal bloom,
> When time, and pain, and nature die.
> I look to heaven's eternal hill,
> To meet that glorious day
> When Christ His promise shall fullfill,
> And call my soul away."

This is the 25th day of December, 1891. On this day nearly nineteen hundred years ago Christ became one by nature and law with man. Hence the lights and shadows of His wonderful history as Son of man—God of seraphim, made flesh and dwelling among men. To do this His eternity was invested with time. His Omnipotence put on frailty. His immensity was subjected to limitation. The Ever-living began to be, and the Source of knowledge learned wisdom. He was found in the real form and structure of a human being, "born of a woman and made under the law," and, in laying aside the grandeur and magnificence of His past eternity, in becoming man, He incurred, for the time, substantial misery and degradation. He who had strewn the path of eternity with the wonders of Omnipotence, and lighted up the mansions of infinity with the emanations of His bounty, became a houseless wanderer in a world of poverty and woe! He who was infinite, unmeasured and unapproached in all His perfections, circumscribed the infinitude of His being to the dimensions of a child. He who had paved the heavens with the blue sky and strewn the earth with flowers—had given to the one its magnificent jewelry and robed the other in vernal loveliness—had not in His humilation where to lay His head. "A body hast thou prepared me," says our Almighty surety, and millions of immortals have hailed, in this single sentence, the kind reversal of their doom. The nativity of Christ is preëminently the display of God's mercy to man. It was a dispensation of kindness meeting us when most we needed aid, and meeting us with the very kindness, which most of all, we needed. And here and thus we have the great and only law of man's return to God. The nativity of Christ,—this God with men, should be the mainspring of every person's happy Christmas.

As I sit here in pain, without a single token of sympathy from the human race, I am profoundly grateful to God for my precious Saviour. That Christ came to save me, reconciles me to the numerous and depressing afflictions of my life. Amid them all, my world is strictly within myself, and its openings look out on immortality. Amid the vexations and disquieting scenes of my earthly suffering, I forget not the song of my pilgrimage, " I live, yet not I, but Christ liveth in me." This thought illumes the darkness without and hallows all within.

> "Shut in, shut in from the ceaseless din
> Of the restless world, and its want and sin ;
> Shut in from its turmoil, care and strife,
> And all the wearisome round of life.
>
> Shut in with tears that are spent in vain,
> With the dreadful companionship of pain ;
> Shut in with the changeless days and hours,
> And the bitter knowledge of failing powers.
>
> Shut in with dreams of the days gone by,
> With buried joys that were born to die ;
> Shut in with hopes that have lost their zest,
> And leave but a longing after rest.

> Shut in with a trio of angels sweet,
> Patience and grace all pain to meet,
> With faith that can suffer, and stand, and wait,
> And lean on the promises strong and great.
>
> Shut in with Christ! O wonderful thought!
> Shut in with the peace His sufferings brought;
> Shut in with the love that wields the rod;
> O company blest! shut in with God."

I have written this short history of my affliction in a perfect agony of pain, but with triumphant faith in my Saviour. He wills that I should weep and continue to endure constant suffering, but my tears shall be like David's who at the lowest point of his fortune plaintively besought God, "Put Thou my tears into Thy bottle," and with the same breath exclaimed, "I will render praises unto Thee." I have had bitterness and trials in abundance, and many hours of sadness, and many hard struggles. But high above these mists and clouds of wailing and grief rises the hope that seeks the skies, and deep beneath all the surface agitations of storms and currents there is the unmoved stillness of the central ocean of peace in my heart. Taking Christ for my Saviour and friend, my guide and support through time, and Himself, my eternity of joy, all discords are reconciled—and "all things are mine," whether the world, or life, or death, or things present, or things to come: all are mine, and I am Christ's and Christ is God's.

"O let the world go on and sing
  Her battle hymns, her victor's crown;
  I throw no knightly gauntlet down,
  Nor join her gay processioning,
  Nor court her smile, nor fear her frown;
  But close to my Saviour's bosom cling."

It is now January the 17th 1892, and my sufferings have become so intense that I must soon have my limb re-amputated or expire with it on me. My friends have requested me to try to endure my sufferings until I record the story of my life—which is now almost completed. The climax of fearful exhaustion and of dreadful pain I feel to be close at hand.

I know that re-amputation is the only remedy in my case, and that it cannot be avoided much longer, but in regard to the result of such an operation the extent of any foresight does not reach beyond probability and amounts to nothing. God in His wisdom saw it not best that I should have the means of anticipating exactly what will happen to me when my leg is taken off the second time. "The hand that beckons us to glory waves us out of impenetrable clouds. We walk in a way we know not. We labor for our Master, but never know beforehand which shall prosper, this or that. We lay wise plans, and they miscarry. We commit gross blunders, and they are overruled for good. We run toward the light, and it goes out in darkness, we stand shivering in the darkness and it turns to light. We pray for joys, and they mildew into griefs. We accept the griefs, and they blossom into joys. To-day the apple turns to ashes, and to-morrow the stones to bread. We exult in some prosperity, and get leanness from it. We murmur at some adversity, and find it big with blessings. We run toward open doors, and dash our head against a granite wall. We move against the wall at the call of duty, and it opens to let us through. The lines of our lives are all in God's hands. What shall befall us, we cannot know. What is expedient we cannot tell. Only this we know, that God would shape us to himself, whether it be by the discipline of joy, or the discipline of sorrow." Many efficient surgeons have told me that my prospects of surviving an operation are exceedingly limited because I am hedged in on every side by serious and complicated disease. Thus situated, I can only trust God and pray.

> " Oh, Father take me by the hand,
> The way is long and I am weak,
> It would be vain to strive with feeble sense
> To pierce the gloom that clouds my path,
> The darkness grows more intense,
> I grope along the narrow way,
> Which leads up to the mountain's height,
> 'Tis dark!' I cannot walk by sight,
> Oh, Father, take me by the hand.

> Oh, Father, take me by the hand,
> And lead me all the weary way;
> Oh let Thy presence like a wall,
> Surround and keep me, day by day,
> Until I tread with blood washed feet,
> The golden avenues of Light
> And in-exchange for feeble faith,
> Receive the glorious gift of sight."

Bidding adieu to the readers of the story of my suffering life, and committing myself, and family and friends, into the tender care of my precious Saviour, and making the guardianship of His presence, the watchfulness of His unslumbering eye, the source of my only hope here, and in the world to come.

I remain, in resignation, peace and faith,

JOSEPH HAMILTON FESPERMAN.

Barium Springs, Iredell County, N. C.

www.ingramcontent.com/pod-product-compliance
Lightning Source LLC
Chambersburg PA
CBHW022143160426
43197CB00009B/1416